Power and Marginality in the Abraham Narrative

Princeton Theological Monograph Series

K. C. Hanson, Charles M. Collier, and
D. Christopher Spinks, Series Editors

Recent volumes in the series

William A. Tooman and Michael A. Lyons
*Transforming Visions: Transformations of Text,
Tradition, and Theology in Ezekiel*

Lowell K. Handy
Psalm 29 through Time and Tradition

Thomas J. King
*The Realignment of the Priestly Literature: The Priestly Narrative in
Genesis and Its Relation to Priestly Legislation and the Holiness School*

Aaron B. Hebbard
Reading Daniel as a Text in Theological Hermeneutics

Matthew J. Marohl
Faithfulness and the Purpose of Hebrews: A Social Identity Approach

Christopher W. Skinner
*John and Thomas—Gospels in Conflict?: Johannine
Characterization and the Thomas Question*

David A. Ackerman
*Lo, I Tell You a Mystery: Cross, Resurrection, and
Paraenesis in the Rhetoric of 1 Corinthians*

Power and Marginality in the Abraham Narrative

Second Edition

HEMCHAND GOSSAI

☙PICKWICK *Publications* • Eugene, Ore

POWER AND MARGINALITY IN THE ABRAHAM NARRATIVE
Second Edition

Princeton Theological Monograph Series 130

Copyright © 2010 Hemchand Gossai. All rights reserved. Except for brief quotations in critical publications or reviews, no part of this book may be reproduced in any manner without prior written permission from the publisher. Write: Permissions, Wipf and Stock Publishers, 199 W. 8th Ave., Suite 3, Eugene, OR 97401.

Pickwick Publications
An Imprint of Wipf and Stock Publishers
199 W. 8th Ave., Suite 3
Eugene, OR 97401

ISBN 13: 978-1-55635-874-6

Cataloging-in-Publication data:

Gossai, Hemchand.

    Power and marginality in the Abraham Narrative / Hemchand Gossai.

    Princeton Theological Monograph Series 130

    xiv + 154 p. ; 23 cm. —Includes bibliographic references.

    ISBN 13: 978-1-55635-874-6

    1. Bible. O.T. Genesis—Criticism, interpretation, etc. 2. Bible. O.T. Judges XIX—Criticism, interpretation, etc. 3. Abraham (Biblical patriarch). 4. Sarah (Biblical matriarch). 5. Hagar (Biblical character). I. Title. II. Series.

BS1235.2 G67 2010

Manufactured in the U.S.A.

For
Chandra, my daughter
A Gift; A Joy

Contents

Acknowledgments / ix

Preface / xi

Abbreviations / xiii

1. A Voice Crying in the Wilderness (Genesis 16; 21:9–21) / 1
2. From Particularity to Universality (Genesis 18) / 25
3. On Choosing Death (Genesis 19) / 55
4. Risking the Future for the Present (Genesis 20) / 81
5. Silence of the Lamb (Genesis 22) / 102
6. Answering Violence with Violence (Judges 19) / 122

Bibliography / 147

Acknowledgments

My sincere thanks to K. C. Hanson for including this volume in the Princeton Theological Monograph series. As is the custom of the staff at Wipf & Stock, careful attention to every detail in the preparation and production of the volume is a trademark, and it is evident.

I am particularly grateful to Walter Brueggemann and Elie Wiesel who read parts of the manuscript and shared their insights generously, and to J. Gerald Janzen who read the entire manuscript and whose comments and insights have made this into a better study.

My life is full being surrounded by Nathan, Krista, Chandra, and Annika.

Preface

THIS STUDY IS BORN OUT OF A CONCERN TO BRING TO BIBLICAL STUDY voices that are not shaped primarily by the conventions of western traditions and cultures. While clearly the theological and philosophical directions shaped by historical methodology have left an indelible stamp on biblical hermeneutics, recently some biblical scholars have probed in different directions and sought to determine new and daring ways of reading the Bible while maintaining the integrity of the text.

The presupposition for this study is that the hermeneutical trajectories that have been traditionally used have not by any means exhausted the possibilities for biblical directions. I have sought to focus on the canonical text and ask questions of it. In the last century or so, the historical reconstruction of the text has dominated biblical scholarship, asking the question, "what really transpired." This study, however, focuses on the final form of the text, asking the questions "now what," "how," and "who."

The Abraham narrative continues to be a source of astounding importance both in the world of biblical scholarship and the church. In interpreting these texts, I have tried to be attentive to the newer methods of biblical interpretation.

I proceed on the premise that the text has a voice and I have employed aspects of literary criticism as a means of re-directing the voice as one that emanates from the margin, rather than the center. The multidimensional nature of power and the prominent issue of marginality are the points of departure for this study. We are continually aware that the Abraham narrative is replete with scenes of confrontation and power struggles. Many of the power struggles take place between parties who do not have the same or even similar levels of power. Moreover, it is the case that often confrontation transpires between those at the center and those on the margin. Mutual confrontation may only legitimately eventuate between parties with power. By definition, those who live and function on the margin are ill equipped to be subjects of confrontation.

Thus when an encounter between center and margin transpires, it is one that reflects a power/powerless dichotomy.

While each of the chapters explored has a life of its own, there is a clear unity within the Abraham narrative, and one of the uniting forces is the consistent role of marginalized persons. While their presence is critical for the ebb and flow of the narrative, and indeed for the denouement, their very identity is subsumed through voicelessness and abuse.

Abbreviations

HBT	*Horizons in Biblical Theology*
Int	*Interpretation*
ISBL	Indiana Studies in Biblical Literature
JBL	*Journal of Biblical Literature*
JBQ	*Jewish Biblical Quarterly*
JNES	*Journal of Near Eastern Studies*
JP	*Journal of Preaching*
JSOT	*Journal for the Study of the Old Testament*
JSOTSup	Journal for the Study of the Old Testament Supplements
MT	Masoretic text
NAB	New American Bible
NIV	New International Version
NJB	New Jerusalem Bible
NRSV	New Revised Standard Version
OBT	Overtures to Biblical Theology
RSV	Revised Standard Version
Tanakh	The Holy Scriptures (JPS)
WW	*Word and World*
ZAW	*Zeitschrift für die alttestamentliche Wissenschaft*

1

A Voice Crying in the Wilderness

Genesis 16; 21:9–21

BOTH THE POSITIONING AND THE NATURE OF THE HAGAR NARRATIVES point to their complexity and far-reaching effect upon the Abraham narratives. One is struck in this narrative by the striking, and sometimes overpowering parallels to contemporary situations in which issues of oppression and the power/powerless dichotomy are present. Some of these parallels will be examined later in connection with specific references. Until the latter part of the twentieth century, the Hagar episodes have not generated significant scholarly attention, but in the several recent decades, primarily through the work of women scholars, some important studies have been done. Within the feminist areas,[1] these episodes have attracted, "the best of the fruits of feminist biblical criticism with its passion for reclaiming and reconstructing the stories of the biblical women, along with the best of Afro-American oral tradition . . ."[2] Moreover, the Hagar narratives have been explored from the perspective of liberation theology.[3]

The reality is that the stories of Hagar in their brevity might easily be subsumed in the Abraham narrative and the conventional focus on the centrality of Abraham. Yet the messages proclaimed therein are distinct and specific and we must ensure that they are never cast aside

---

1. Trible, *Texts of Terror*. Trible was a pioneer in bringing to the fore serious feminist-literary work on the biblical material with her acclaimed work, *God and the Rhetoric of Sexuality*. Also, Darr, *Far More Precious than Jewels*; Fuchs, "The Literary Characterization"; Jeansonne, *The Women of Genesis*; and Teubal, *Hagar the Egyptian*.

2. Weems, *Just a Sister Away*.

3. Tamez, "The Woman."

or relegated to a place on the margin. The Hagar episodes with their far-reaching implications move the Abraham narratives away from the particular focus on the "faith of Abraham" into the realm of other universal themes.

The narrative in Genesis 16 begins with the naming of three characters, Sarai, Abram and Hagar. With immediacy in the first two verses, the problem is named, responsibility for Sarai's barrenness is ascribed to Yahweh, and the solution is sought in the person of Hagar, the fertile Egyptian slave woman.[4]

States of Powerlessness: Center to Margin

It has been noted, and will be repeatedly, that Sarai, like all the women in the Old Testament lived within an intensely patriarchal system.[5] To be sure, it was a challenging system for all women. However, what is frequently overlooked are the many rings which constitute the ever expanding states of powerlessness in our society.[6] While Sarai functions within a patriarchal system, she is however on a different social and economic level than Hagar and thus it is not helpful and certainly not accurate to speak "simply about the women" of the Bible as some kind of monolithic entity. Many levels of oppression and poverty exist, and to reduce all of the oppressed and marginalized into one common category, is to instill yet another ring of suffering.[7] If Sarai represents

---

4. Trible observes, "Beginning with Sarai and ending with Hagar, the narrated introduction opposes two women around the man Abram," *Texts of Terror*, 10.

5. Schüssler Fiorenza, "Emerging Issues in Feminist Biblical Interpretation": "Patriarchy defines not just women as the 'other' but it defines also the subjugated peoples and races as the 'other' to be dominated. Moreover, it defines women not just as the other of men, but also as subjugated to men in power insofar as it conceives of society in analogy to the patriarchal household that was sustained by slave labor. Women of color and poor women are doubly and triply oppressed in such a patriarchal societal system," 37.

6. Weems, *Just a Sister Away*, 8, places this matter in a contemporary situation: "White women within feminist and christian feminist circles continue to speak as though theirs is the universal experience. In doing so, they betray their persistent belief in their superiority and sovereignty over women of other races." See also, hooks, *Feminist Theory*. Hooks provides a sharp and incisive evaluation and critique of feminism as espoused by white women.

7. See Brock, *Journeys by Heart*, who notes that, "Schüssler Fiorenza contend(s) that women represent, at least in some of the biblical stories, the marginal in society . . . As metaphors of exclusion, the women represent those who have been denied admission

the center of oppressed people, then surely Hagar represents those who are on the periphery.[8] One of the very troubling features of this type of gradation is that the oppressed begin to treat other oppressed people who are at a different level, with concomitant disdain and contempt as they received.

Even though Sarai is the one who takes the initiative, we note in v. 1a, that she is "Abram's wife" and her action is in fact prompted by the absence of children *borne for him*. The narrator establishes at the outset that power is gauged by familial and societal status. Hagar's youth and fertility are a secondary matter. For Sarai, at this juncture in her life, these characteristics serve to remind her of what she is not, and serve as legal props in aiding her. In the eyes of Sarai, Hagar simply provides for her something missing in her own life over which she has no control. In the estimation of Sarai, the One who *does* have control, has chosen not to exercise that control by granting her the fulfillment she seeks. There is no inkling in Sarai's plan that Hagar's identity will be any different from its present status, and certainly nothing hints that there will be a fundamental transformation in Hagar after conception. Moreover, Sarai's one-dimensional plan clearly leaves no room for the possibility of a new future with a transformed Hagar.[9] Sarai's fundamental interest centers on herself and the furthering of her own identity and recognition. The

---

to or full participation . . . on the basis of factors over which authorities and experts have no power," 85. Also, Chopp, *The Power to Speak*, 15, who notes that "marginal also means the effacing of women, for women are not men, and hence are really present and can be overlooked: in this sense marginal means having no substance, containing nothing, the emptiness of the margins. Marginal also implies also the notion of the borderline or limit or edge, as margin defines the edges of a text. Here women are cast as the border—literally, the margin—which demarcates order and chaos. As the border of the social-symbolic order take on characteristics of the chaos so feared by the order, but as outer rim of the order, women can take on characteristics revered by the order."

8. See Bettenhausen, "Hagar Revisited." Using the story of Hagar as a framework for speaking about the specific case of baby M and the Court's decision, Bettenhausen says, "There is no difference between Aristotle's notion that the sperm contained the entire child in miniature and . . . the view that baby M belonged to the father alone. In both cases, the woman is seen as an embodied uterus, convenient for patriarchy. Sarah was caught in this trap; Hagar had no choice being a slave," 159. Whether Bettenhausen intended it or not, she does point to the differing states of powerlessness within the large category of the oppressed. See also, Tamez, who observes, that Hagar, "is a person oppressed three times over, owing to her slave status, her race and her sex," "The Woman," 8.

9. See Trible, *Texts of Terror*, 11: "For Sarai, Hagar is an instrument, not a person. The maid enhances the mistress."

phrase, "I shall be built up through her,"(16:2a) indicates Sarai's intent clearly. "The strange pun on <*ibbaneh* ('I will build up through her' or 'I will get sons through her') . . . suggests that the matriarch's desire is less for the proper construing of God's intent to multiply descendants than it is for the construction of a monument to herself. Shades of the tower of Babel. And her babble—her idea of confusing not mother tongues, but mothers—wins Abram's ear.[10]

Sarai's actions do not indicate that the promise expressed to Abram earlier is at the heart of her initiative. Nor is any thought given to Abram or Hagar in this sentiment, though both of them will subsequently be blamed for the episode. As if to highlight further the differences in power, Hagar the slave woman, is never consulted. It is assumed that Hagar, as a slave, is entirely at the disposal of her mistress. Sarai was demonstrating that she was capable of achieving that which Yahweh had naturally prevented her from doing (v. 2a).

Like Sarai, Hagar surely understands the importance of an heir and while their realities are radically different, one from the other, nonetheless in the present they share the common reality of no realistic prospect for an heir. However, given her status as slave, with no framework for an opportunity of an offspring, she holds tightly to the chance that she has at her disposal. Even though the decision to use Hagar treats her as a non-entity, the occasion opens for Hagar a dream which she dared not have dreamt before: the unthinkable becomes thinkable and the impossible appears possible. While Sarai considers the occasion a way of building herself up, she fails to consider that the slave woman might also have such daring hopes for herself. But then how could a free person fathom the reality of a slave! That Hagar would want to build herself up is simply never entertained. That is all the more troubling, and it reflects the dire straits of a slave who is *ipso facto* also an "outsider." Under any circumstances, a slave holds little or no power and has a narrow future, though in the case of Israelite slaves, there was the opportunity for manumission.[11] For Hagar, an Egyptian, there was no such built-in legal containment. The encounter between Sarai and

10. Brisman, *The Voice of Jacob*, 52. See also the Tanakh, which notes that to "be built up" is a play on *ben* "son" and *banah* "build up," 22.

11. See, e.g., Exod 21:2–4; Lev 25:44–46; Deut 15:12. In the modern era, indentured servants were given the opportunity for manumission after a designated time of service to their masters. With no land, wealth, home, most indentured servants found this "legal freedom" only in theory, not in reality.

Hagar redefined the nature of human value outside of socio-cultural status. Hagar's status as a slave, in and of itself, was an insufficient basis for the shaping and determining of her personhood.

Given today's religio-cultural norms, Sarai's actions in arranging for a sexual relationship between Abram and Hagar would likely prompt serious disapproval. Strangely enough, some religious quarters seeking to "protect" Sarai have deemed her actions proper, given her intentions. By and large however, there is confusion and not a little reproof by some contemporary religious folks.[12] Yet, what Sarai did was legal, and indeed acceptable in the Ancient Near East.[13] In sharp contrast to the typical condemnation of Sarai's sexual scenario, there is very little that is said regarding the devastating matter of slavery, which is in fact the framework through which Sarai is able to act. It is troublesome that slavery, as a reprehensible expression of dehumanization is rarely found to be a debatable issue when this text is considered or a central point of departure for any discussion about the issue of power in light of Sarai's actions. It might be argued that the matter between Hagar and Sarai, as important as it is, is but the symptom of a larger systemic oppression, and by dealing with the sexual matter, the greater violence is overlooked.

Upon occasion individuals, communities or nations are so consumed with the sustaining of the legal tradition that injustice is promulgated under the protection of the law. Legal requirements often instill fear, much the opposite to the intent of the law. When injustice and oppression are concealed under the guise of "keeping the law," or functioning within the limits of the law, then the need to review the intent of the legal tradition is long overdue.[14] The intent of the law is typically not an invitation to oppress and create artificial superiority and class

12. See Wiesel, "Ishmael and Hagar." Wiesel, in characteristic manner, gets to the heart of the matter and says, "If we try hard we can exonerate Sarah. But apologies no longer have a place in our tradition . . . The patriarchs are neither infallible saints nor angels. They are human beings with impulses of grandeur and weakness," 248.

13. See, e.g., *The Code of Hammurabi* §146, which notes that a mistress may give her female slave to her husband for reproduction. Also, Speiser, *Genesis*. However, along with the legal permission granted by the CH, Sarai's action in casting out Hagar and Ishmael is forbidden (§170).

14. Haughton, *The Passionate God*, 12, observes that, "If an explanation is easily and smoothly acceptable in any particular culture the chances are great that its terms are culturally conditioned—that is, adapted to the expectations and subliminal exclusions of that society, and so designed to provide reassurance rather than the challenge of real exploratory thinking."

systems. Sarai's treatment of Hagar was clearly within the restraints of ancient Near East legal traditions and the societal customs that surrounded her. But what of the particular injustice perpetrated against Hagar as a person? What of the dehumanizing of Hagar? As injustices become more prominent, invariably they become established and acceptable as norms. Whether in the case of slavery or other forms of oppression, the reality is that any established norm is difficult to erode and erase. Even though slavery has been abolished in this land, the scars on society as a whole clearly persist.

While the immediate issue at stake in this narrative is centered on the quest for a son, and the ends to which Sarai pursued this, a larger matter calls us to recognize the fact that the "outsider" is used to fulfill the needs and desires of the "insider." The use of Hagar goes beyond surrogacy, beyond ethnicity and tradition. So strong is Sarai's urge for a child that she is willing to overlook any such issue regarding Hagar. Moreover, to be a slave is to be fully owned. There is, in reality no component in a slave's life which belongs exclusively to the slave. The entire being of the slave is at the disposal of the owner. More than anything, Hagar as an "outsider" needed hospitality from the community in general, and from Sarai and Abram in particular under whose roof she finds herself. As if being a slave were not demeaning enough, Hagar is the object of additional hostility by her mistress. As we shall see from Sarai's actions, fear leads to hostility. Note three points in this regard.

First, the indifference to Hagar as a person in her own right is seen throughout the narrative. Even though Sarai is the one who initiates the plan, she never refers to Hagar by name.[15] It is the narrator who names Hagar. Thus, at the outset, Hagar's identity is made incomplete or perhaps more accurately undermined through Sarai's reference by description of "slave" or "servant" as to her name. The name is at the heart and soul of the person; it is in some significant respects a quintessential expression of identity. Through a name one is told who the person is and one is invited to have knowledge of them and experience them. It is not insignificant that the term "boy" was used to refer to black male

---

15. Teubal, *Hagar the Egyptian*, 73ff., argues that for ten years the relationship between Sarai and Hagar was a good one, and Sarai's decision to have a child through Hagar was only the first occasion in which Hagar is called upon to do something out of the ordinary. Textually, Teubal's position seems untenable; yet, if there is tenability in what she says, then Sarai's reference to Hagar is all the more surprising.

slaves, and numbers and symbols are yet used to identify prisoners.[16] The stark and telling difference between human and divine recognition of one's personhood is seen in 16:8, where Hagar is addressed by name by the angel of Yahweh. Even as a slave, an outsider, an oppressed person, Hagar has an identity that is divinely given.

Second, not only is Hagar not consulted nor spoken to by Sarah, she is entirely without voice. She is not allowed to cry out against the double injustice of concubinage and slavery done to her; she is muted by the two sources of power between whom she is caught. The reality is that she is without voice, unable to speak a language of power and domination, and has no advocate as her vision remains one from the outside looking in. The oppressed is left voiceless. The only voice in these opening verses is that of Sarai and she orders Abram to act. Abram, who is clearly in a position to decide justly what is right and wrong, listens to the voice of power and proceeds from that point. Clearly the issue of Hagar's silence has far-reaching implications. The irony is that the poor and powerless, arguably more than any other disenfranchised group need a voice, and they are the ones who are made voiceless thus adding to their state of marginalization.

Invariably, whether in a particular case, or in a systemic situation, being "gagged" always implies a hiding of truth. One cannot read of Hagar's situation and not think of those who live among us, who are oppressed and voiceless. Who will advocate on their behalf? Not to speak on behalf of the voiceless is in no way an expression of neutrality, but in reality a pronouncement of hostility.[17] While it is Sarai who speaks and Abram who obeys, he remains in a position of power, and consequently should have been the voice of the silent. He is not; he, like Sarai wittingly or unwittingly participates in a hostile and oppressive act.

Third, the use of Hagar underlines the premise that the entire being of the slave is legally at the disposal of the owner. Hagar powerfully exemplifies this premise. By deciding that Abram will "lie" with Hagar, Sarai makes clear her ownership of the womb of Hagar. The fact that Hagar is never consulted further testifies this. The sharp irony here is

---

16. See Heger, *The Men with the Pink Triangle*. In telling the story of one homosexual prisoner under the Nazis, we are provided with a glimpse into the manner in which homosexuals were treated in Nazi concentration camps, including identification through the wearing of pink triangles.

17. We think of the voiceless woman in Judges 19. She waited for an hospitable advocate and received hostility and death instead.

that Sarai expresses emptiness of the womb in more than one way. The Hebrew root *rḥm* (womb) is also the term typically translated "compassion" in the Hebrew Bible (e.g., Lam 4:10; Isa 27:11). Trible suggests that, "the root *rḥm* unites these themes; the place of birth is the vehicle of compassion. To create is to love."[18] Sarai demonstrates in this instance that she is lacking in compassion and even at the sight of the two sons at play, instead of joy and compassion, she feels fear and jealousy (Gen 21:9ff.). Sarai's lack of compassion is contrasted with Yahweh's compassion. Indeed, Yahweh's creative powers come to the fore, as through the messenger, Hagar is shown compassion and hospitality.

Esteem or Contempt?

Given Sarai's role as a central matriarch in the patriarchal narratives, we are not surprised that despite her actions against Hagar, some scholars, both ancient and modern, hold her to be without blemish. There is a sense that, despite the clarity of the text, Sarai's character must be protected even at the expense of pursuing the truth of her directives. Indeed, Sarai's very action in making Abram take Hagar as a wife is euphemized by some. Westermann suggests that "Sarah's demand 'Go then to my maidservant!' means just what it says—Abraham is to turn to Hagar, spend part of his time with her, so there arises a mutual understanding between them."[19] Westermann's conclusion appears untenable in the light of Sarai's very sharp, to the point instructions. Saraiís intentions are designed for her personal welfare, not for that of Abram.

The absence of an understanding of the transformation effected by conception, leads to the conflict with Hagar. Here again, the blame is often cast on Hagar. The NRSV renders v. 4b as "she looked with contempt on her mistress."[20] The Tanakh says, "her mistress was lowered in her esteem." With conception, Hagar discovered an esteem for herself that comes with creation. The issue is not contempt for Sarai, but rather

---

18. Trible, *God and the Rhetoric of Sexuality*, 55.
19. Westermann, *Genesis 12–36*, 239.
20. See also, NEB, NJB, NAB all of which render similar translations of this verse. Sarai is established as the victim. See also, Janzen, "Hagar in Paul's Eyes." He argues that, "it is not Hagar, but Sarai, that is the subject of the verb (which comes from the root *qll* . . .)," 5.

a recognition of a source of power and love.[21] The occasion provides for Hagar a source of hitherto unknown power. However, as important as this power is, and Sarai *does* recognize its importance, it cannot be equated with the power which comes through wealth and ownership. Hagar's newly discovered esteem is not greeted with any delight by Sarai. Hagar, who without regard was given to Abram, has become a source of despair for Sarai.[22] Trible notes, "Unwittingly, Sarai has contributed to Hagar's insight. By giving Hagar to Abram for a wife, Sarai hoped to be built up. In fact, however, she has enhanced the status of the servant to become herself correspondingly lowered in the eyes of Hagar."[23] Thus, what transpired was doubly painful for Sarai, for not only was she not built up, but she built up in Hagar a person over whom she could never again have absolute control. The potential for diminishing is only in the eyes of Sarai. It is inconceivable, that a slave-woman, a foreigner, voiceless, without advocate, without family, would be a challenge and threat to the established power reflected in the persons of Sarai and Abram. Undeniably, there is a source of strength and hope in having an offspring, though this is not to be equated with systemic and covenantal power.

In contemporary society, it is not altogether surprising that members of the poorer classes, and people of poorer nations have more children; whatever criticism is leveled against this practice typically comes from those who enjoy power through financial, political, social or economic status and perhaps in a state of plenty. While it might seem incongruous that poorer families have many children, the inherent perception of power and hope for the future invites the poor to have large families. Conventionally, wealthy families with no anxiety regarding power and continuance have fewer children.

---

21. See Van Seters, *Abraham in History and Tradition*, who concludes that, "when Hagar, the maid-slave becomes pregnant she adopts a haughty manner towards her mistress and makes life intolerable for her," 192.

22. Wiesel who suggests that, "Hagar meant no disrespect toward her mistress; it is Sarah who imagines terrible things of that sort. In other words, Hagar is Sarah's victim and Sarah was wrong to impose a role on upon her and then begrudge her for playing it too well," "Ishmael and Hagar," 228.

23. Trible, *Texts of Terror*, 12.

Who Is to Blame? Who Is to Judge!

While Sarai is fearful of the newly transformed Hagar, she is not willing to recognize fully her own initiative and responsibility in the matter. The issue is no longer the longing for a child, but a challenge to the status quo and those who constitute the status quo. Some recognize the power in Hagar, which is absent in Sarai, and at this point in her life beyond the latter's reach. That Sarai's interest in an offspring now assumes a secondary role is displayed by her willingness and interest in dismissing Hagar and the unborn child. Challenge of power becomes the crux at this point in the narrative. If ever there was the notion that Sarai was led by the importance of the promise, it is erased here. Sarai's quest to retaliate against Hagar affirms her jealousy of a power which Hagar owns, and she is unable to attain.

Despite Abram's passive role in the planning of the event, when Sarai feels slighted by Hagar, Abram receives the blame. In Sarai's estimation, Abram is the cause of her perceived loss of power, though the narrator refrains from supporting Sarai in this conclusion.[24] Indeed Abram recognizes the matter for what it is worth and tells Sarai to act according to what she considers right.

Sarai never asks Abram to punish or to act harshly with Hagar. In fact Sarai simply recognizes the differing alignment of power between Hagar and herself. Moreover, Sarai comes to the conclusion that she is not willing to share Abram with Hagar, and consequently seeks to rectify the earlier order to have Hagar be Abram's wife (v. 3). The state-

---

24. Teubal argues that the anger voiced by Sarai is not directed at Abram. "The matriarch's first words of admonishment to Abraham are *ḥamasi aleha* . . . *Ḥamasi aleha* is more than an invocation of Sarai's legal rights, however, because the phrase is a kind of curse. What Sarai is actually saying to Abraham is: 'That I am deprived of my right is on you!' . . . Although Abraham's infraction is not clearly defined, the text seems to indicate that Abraham's behavior generated doubt regarding Sarah's claim to Hagar's child. Sarah's severe reproach must have stemmed from the terms of an accord or contract that Abraham has breached. Abraham's offense, deserving of malediction, was his intent to override the authority of the matriarch by instigating the rebellion of Hagar, *thus attempting to deprive Sarah of her legal right to an heir*," *Hagar the Egyptian*, 79–80. As interesting and imaginative as Teubal's reconstruction is, the text does not support such a thesis. Similarly see, Tsevat, *The Meaning of the Book of Job*. "[Abraham], the master of the house, is permitting her handmaid to infringe on her position as mistress. As he has failed her, Sarai, in providing the protection due to her, this has become a case between her and him, and let God be the judge. Hagar, who has caused the trouble, is, at this point not herself a litigant, more a circumstance than a protagonist," 55.

ment, "May the Lord judge between you and me!" is significant. It is, in this statement that Sarai expresses her interest. While the overtone is judicial, the fundamental issue at stake is restoration and reconciliation between Sarai and Abram. Sarai's statement is not for Yahweh to determine who is to be blamed. Rather, it is a statement which calls for the healing of the relationship between Sarai and Abram. The Hebrew *špṭ* found in this verse not only has a forensic meaning in the Hebrew Bible, but as the noun *mišpaṭ* indicates, it is that justice which is intrinsic to a proper relationship. Abram recognizes the issue at stake and while he does not himself respond actively to the blame laid on him by Sarai, he concludes that Hagar, as the slave-woman must take the responsibility.

Verse 6 generally begins with "but," suggesting an adversative element in the response, and thereby leading to Abram's refusal to accept the responsibility laid on him. However, a more appropriate translation of the Hebrew *waw* in this context is "and." In this way, Abram's response reflects his interest in sustaining the relationship with Sarai, and in so doing compounds the blame against Hagar.

The troublesome factor in the resolution revolves around a pronouncement determined by the powerful against the powerless, where the powerless is without voice. Moreover, the innocent person is Hagar, the powerless. In the face of condemnation, she is not recognized. Abram's response in v. 6 includes four critical elements, all of which factor into the oppression against Hagar.

First, it is odd that Abram is the one who has to give permission to Sarai, and stranger perhaps since she did not explicitly ask for permission.[25] From the text, Sarai does not need permission. In fact the statement, "your slave-girl is in your hands" (power), is more a reminder than a permission. Moreover, it is a reminder that Sarai does indeed have the kind of power as mistress that allows her to suppress the esteem of Hagar and place her again in an absolutely subservient role. It is to be noted also, that once the reminder is made to Sarai, there is no discussion or argument on her part.

---

25. Westermann notes that Abraham "confirms Hagar's status and consequently allows Sarah freedom of action. The confirmation reestablishes the former situation . . . and the permission allows Sarah a free hand in her conduct towards Hagar," *Genesis 12–36*, 241. One notes that language of "allowing" and "permitting" suggests that it is Abram who is in charge in this situation. In the light of Sarai's initiative in the first place, coupled with Abram's passivity, Westermann's conclusion seems implausible.

Second, Abram assures Sarai that she has the power to do that which is *good in her eyes*. This is essentially a *carte blanche* statement to use one's power. With Hagar in a powerless state and cast into the role of instigator, Hagar is left without recourse. Abram must be saddled with responsibility here as he is aware of the fear and anger of Sarai, and still he suggests that she determine the nature of the punishment, on the basis of what she considers good! Essentially Abram washes his hand of the matter and allows Sarai to be the one to have "hands stained with blood." Sarai, like Lady Macbeth began this scenario with a plan in mind, and as the plot disintegrates, it is Sarai who has blood-stained hands. On the other hand, Abram like Pilate attempts to "wash his hands" of the matter, though by not acting with his inherent power, he is deeply embroiled in the episode and is himself responsible. As opposed to the objective *mišpaṭ*, which is the essence of a proper relationship, it is the *ṭob* as determined by a slighted Sarai that will be meted out to Hagar. Even before witnessing the result of Sarai's actions, one is placed on alert by Sarai's previous action in inviting Abram to lie with Hagar. We are aware that she might be incapable of dealing wisely and fairly with Hagar. Whatever else one might think of Sarai in this context, she is not in a position to make a good judgment.[26] As a slave, it is clear that Hagar was not Sarai's equal, and the first remote sign of equal status between the two created an overtly adversarial atmosphere. Trible perceptively notes that the situation was primed for further estrangement: "Inequality, opposition and distance breed violence."[27]

Third, Sarai determined that doing what was *good in her eyes* meant dealing harshly with Hagar. This is clearly over and above the harsh treatment which is the lot of the slave under ordinary circumstances. The Hebrew '*nh* translated "afflict" implies severe harshness. As Trible observes, this is the term used in characterizing the harsh treatment of the Hebrews in Egypt.[28] Self-evident is the irony that Hagar as the Egyptian slave is the precursor of the Hebrew in bondage. The subjection of a person or people to affliction is not merely a fleeting experience, but lives within the afflicted for a lifetime and is carried on from generation

---

26. A puissant parallel here is Gen 19:8b, where Lot tells the men of Sodom to do with his daughters that which is "good in their eyes," the identical phrase used by Abram to Sarai.

27. Trible, *Texts of Terror*, 13.

28. Ibid., 13.

to generation (e.g., Deut 26:6). Moreover, to afflict (*'nh*) involves more than physical enslavement.

Elsa Tamez notes that with regard to the affliction of the Hebrews in Egypt, "It touched their inner selves, the transcendental part of their being, their dignity, their persons. It represented a degradation of the human being, a seizure as it were of the divine image in the person . . . That is to say that oppression or exploitation (*'anah*) is accompanied by human degradation and humiliation. It is precisely this oppression, reaching to the innermost self, which moves the God of the Hebrews."[29] Moreover, Abram has been told by Yahweh that his descendants will indeed be afflicted while they are slaves in a foreign land (Gen 15:13) and Abram does not object to Sarai's treatment of Hagar.

Fourth, Hagar in the face of danger flees for her life, and in effect freedom.[30] Given the choice of slavery with a compounded amount of oppression and affliction, Hagar chooses to leave and take the risk of the unknown. It is not unusual that in instances where alternatives appear to run between "a rock and a hard place," one will summon enough courage to pursue freedom. In the case of Hagar, her presence in the household of Sarai moved from a state of tolerance to open hostility. Westermann suggests that, "Hagar's flight into the desert from 'legal' oppression by Sarah, exposing herself to all the dangers involved, is a prime example of the human will for freedom."[31] It is unlikely that Hagar entertained any clear-cut notion of the quest for freedom, but pushed to the limit, the wilderness offered life.[32]

---

29. Tamez, *Bible of the Oppressed*, 12. It is instructive to note that *'nh* is also found in the contexts of the rape of women and it is perhaps these instances which call attention to the extreme nature of the affliction against Hagar. See, e.g., Gen 34:2; 2 Sam 13:12; Judg 19:24.

30. See Hampson, "On Power and Gender," who suggests that, "the process of exodus is the process of empowerment. It is the coming of a new reality," 242. Even though Hagar would return to the place of enslavement, the journey of empowerment has begun.

31. Westermann, *Genesis 12–36*, 242. Also, Wiesel articulates, "When Sarah is hard on [Hagar], she chooses freedom. She goes into the desert—the desert she knows, for it is her homeland. The desert, to her, means total freedom—for her imagination, for her dreams, for her memories. Better to die in the desert—in freedom—then to live in security and in servitude," "Ishmael and Hagar," 243.

32. Westermann argues for a parallel between the actions of Sarah at the start of the story, and Hagar's initiative to flee. "The first part begins with an independent act of one woman, the second with the independent act of another. Sarah's action was justified; her plan could have succeeded. Hagar's action was of desperation; it had no choice."

Promise in the Midst of Despair

Hagar's resting place in the wilderness is by a spring of water, the first sign that she will have life in the face of the uncertainty of the wilderness. It is here that Hagar encounters the divine. Even to this point in the narrative, Hagar remains anonymous (to Abram and Sarai), and voiceless. The encounter between Hagar and Yahweh evokes parallels between Yahweh and the Hebrews during their wilderness experience as they fled from bondage in Egypt. Unlike Moses who called out to Yahweh for water, water is provided for Hagar without her calling. In her state of voicelessness, she is nevertheless provided for. Remarkably, Hagar, unlike Moses, is a rank outsider who is oppressed and afflicted. For all oppressed people this encounter provides a basis for hope and life; Yahweh will indeed hear the silent cries of all people.[33]

Whether it is the silent cry of Hannah (1 Samuel 1) or the cries of the millions who are suffering in a variety of ways around the world today, deliverance is not based on nationality, ethnicity or social status (Amos 9:7). As we see in the case of Hagar, deliverance does not presuppose a particular religious orientation. To be sure, even with the severe treatment of Hagar, neither Sarai nor Abram is reprimanded or punished, but neither is Hagar abandoned. Human power continues in the face of oppression, even as God hears the oppressed. The esteem of Hagar challenged the status of Sarai, and rather than celebrate the transformation of another person, Sarai greets her slave with hostility.[34]

The silence of the text regarding the hardships of a pregnant woman, alone, fleeing to an unknown destination, underlines the dire straits

---

Genesis 12–36, 242. It would appear that it is the reverse of Westermann's thesis that is tenable. Indeed Sarah's action is one of desperation and without any contemplation of the potential change in Hagar's status, it was doomed to failure. Hagar, on the other hand, made a decisive move that was clearly justified in the light of the affliction.

33. While in modern society, it is not typical to hear stories of God "hearing" the cries of the silent, there is evidence that the voiceless exist in large numbers, and are heard only by those who seek to end oppression and misery. For a poignant description of one such story, see, Doig, *Mother Teresa*. Doig details a story titled, "The Child that Could not Cry," who, like Hagar, an abandoned and oppressed outsider, is given life.

34. See Gutierrez, *The Power of the Poor in History*. Speaking to the role of the poor in the Latin American Church, Gutierrez says, "The most significant fact in the political and church life of Latin America in recent years is the active presence that the poor are coming to assume in it. As can be imagined, this does not fail to provoke fear and hostility," 131.

and aloneness of Hagar. The human abandonment is matched by divine care; the hostile environment of Sarai's household is countered by the "hospitable" setting of the wilderness. Hagar's experience as one afflicted overturns the natural order of things. The wilderness experience signals a new beginning for Hagar. As much as the wilderness has come to be identified with hardship and all that is difficult, it is also the place for the encounter with the divine, and regardless of the inherent dangers that the physical wilderness poses, this is a time for newness. The wilderness experience brings an identity to Hagar as Yahweh calls her by name (Isa 43:1). More than simply a place to hide, the wilderness is a metaphor for shaping a new identity and the commencement of a new journey (Hos 2:14; Matt 4:1).

Yahweh does what Abram and Sarai fail to do, namely enters into conversation with Hagar. Westermann suggests "by the greeting and inquiry, the messenger takes part in Hagar's lot; he accepts her into the realm of *shalom*. He enables her to make a trustful response and show herself ready to accept the word of this stranger. That this unknown one speaks her name indicates that he is an 'other,' one who knows; his friendly attention to Hagar evokes her trustful reply."[35] The questioning by the messenger of Yahweh reveals that Hagar has an identity, but it is tied to Sarai. It is true as Trible remarks that the questions by the messenger "embody origin and destiny."[36] Yet Hagar's answer suggests that there is no place of origin, but a slave owner from whom she is fleeing; and there is no certainty of destination and her presence in the wilderness testifies to this. Hagar the slave-woman has become a refugee, fleeing injustice and caught in a purgatorial world. The messenger recognizes that Hagar's destiny is tied to Sarai; as painful as it is, that is the reality. Thus, the issue at stake is one of restoration and reconciliation in the midst of inequities, injustice and power struggles (Matt 26:51–52). When Yahweh orders Hagar to return and submit to Sarai, one is led to conclude that Yahweh is acting on the side of the powerful and seeking to uphold the status quo. At one level it does not appear to make much sense, particularly given the overall direction of the biblical material that places God unquestionably on the side of the poor.

It is not difficult to draw parallels between the sending back of Hagar to Sarai and the plight of modern day refugees. Common to our

35. Westermann, *Genesis 12–36*, 244.
36. Trible, *Texts of Terror*, 15.

existence is the presence of political and economic refugees, huddled together in boats and warehouses, held in barracks and foreign lands; and having spent time in this "in-between" world, they told that they must return to their place of origin. There appears to be no justice when humans are forced by other humans, shaped by power structures, to remain in bondage. So what does the encounter between Hagar and Yahweh establish? Note four points in this regard.

First, Hagar never challenges or questions the messenger's pronouncements. In the light of the recent tortuous experiences of Hagar, and now these words from a hitherto unknown God, her response is truly remarkable. Hagar was never an "insider," which would have been all the more reason for not listening to Yahweh, especially since this is the God of Abram and Sarai.

Second, the future of Hagar, which includes a son and many descendants, will be forged out of a life of submission and slavery. In the face of hostility, Hagar will not only survive, but live, and be destined for a future, albeit through her son. The description of Ishmael's nature demonstrates that he will in fact not live like his mother as a slave. As Ishmael grows in the household of Sarai and Abram, he must have been aware of the oppression that he and his mother faced. One cannot help but conclude that this kind of oppression and affliction are intrinsic in shaping children as they grow into adulthood. As is so often the case, the one who is the recipient of oppression learns that this is the way to live and survive. The conflict that will come to characterize the life of Ishmael can be explained through the experience in the Sarai/Abram household.

Third, the return of Hagar to Sarai is not a return to the status quo. While the messenger's words might appear to be a reconstruction of an identical slave/mistress relationship as existed before, in fact Hagar is now aligned with a different source of power. Hagar now has the confidence of Yahweh, and while Sarai and Abram are covenanted with Yahweh, Yahweh's "preferential option" for the poor is evident here.

Fourth, regarding the return of Hagar to Sarai, Tamez postulates:

> What God wants is that she and her child should be saved, and at the moment the only way to accomplish that is not in the desert, but by returning to the house of Abraham. Ishmael hasn't been born. The first three years of life are crucial. Hagar must wait a little longer because Ishmael must be born in the house of Abraham to prove that he is the first born (Deut. 21:15–17), and

to enter into the household through the rite of circumcision. (Chap. 17) This will guarantee him participation in the history of salvation, and will give rights of inheritance in the house of Abraham.[37]

Hagar who left Sarai's household in fear, returns still as slave, but with a new confidence.[38] We are never told that she is given any new voice in the household or for that matter that she is treated with any greater decency and civility; finally, however those elements will not be intrinsic to the identity that she bears. She returns with a promise and therein lies hope for the future. Even though the promise is not made in the context of a covenant,[39] it nevertheless contains many of the elements of the promise made to Abram and Sarai. There is an unknown factor regarding the future, yet there is a concreteness in the promise to Hagar, in that she is already pregnant. The promise to Abram and Sarai will continue to necessitate faith in a future that appears bleak. Moreover, like Moses and Miriam and Aaron, the promise of deliverance and a future will come to Hagar in the midst of bondage and suffering.

Furthermore, the annunciation by the messenger aligns Hagar with other biblical women to whom such an announcement has come. In particular, Hagar is comparable to Mary, who like Hagar confesses her servanthood (Luke 1:38). There is a recognition of conception, confirmation that a son will be born, the name of the son, significance of the name and a promise of a future through the son.[40] As was the case with Mary, the focus of the annunciation is primarily on the son, not on Hagar. The present reality of Hagar's suffering is hidden and even neglected for the future through Ishmael.[41] This is a consistent trend

37. Tamez, "The Woman," 14.

38. Janzen constructs an imaginative framework for understanding the angel's admonition and Hagar's return. He notes, "Hagar is here asked to engage in an act of moral imagination which will both transcend her customary consciousness and its informing social context, and bring her back into that context. If she will exercise her middle power in the way she is bidden, she will become subject to Sarai without losing her own subjectivity. She will be morally and spiritually free." "Hagar in Paul's Eyes," 12.

39. Trible, *Texts of Terror*, 17.

40. Fuchs suggests that the biblical annunciation type-scene includes the initial barrenness of the wife. "The Literary Characterization of Mothers and Sexual Politics in the Hebrew Bible," p. 119. This seems untenable, not only in the Hagar story, but it is surely not consistently the case in the biblical material.

41. Fuchs notes, "The best consolation offered to Hagar, who has been driven by Sarah, refers not to herself but to her son . . . This consolation which focuses exclusively

in promises made by Yahweh. Abraham would endanger the future through his selfish protection of the present (Genesis 12, 20). The proper tension between the fulfillment of the present and the hope for the future is perfectly characterized in the temptation of Jesus, where the absolute and essential needs of the present are sacrificed for the sake of the promise (Matt 4:1–11).

The naming of Ishmael might very well have embodied the greatest promise. The particularity of Ishmael's name bears a universal promise to all who cry to God. In the midst of the circumstances of life, *God hears* (Ishmael) is a real promise. Yet, this is a hope that must exist in the realm of human power structures. The promise is one not seeking to eliminate the sources of power (imperial, economic, political, etc.) but functioning confidently within these structures. There is nothing facile about the promise. It will, in fact, necessitate courage. In this way, there continues to be a tension between suffering and hope. The suffering of Jesus is the highwater mark of this tension. Moreover, the naming of Ishmael is pre-figured through the response of Abram to Sarai's command to lie with Hagar.

Abram obeying/understanding (*vayyišmaʿ*) Sarai's state of powerlessness through her barrenness, hears her cries and acts without question or complaint, even though finally, he is the one in the household with final power. But Sarai as a powerless person, nevertheless does have a certain amount of power to control others (Hagar); correspondingly, this limited power is reflected in the limited nature of Abram's understanding of powerlessness. In contrast to this, it is in the encounter between Yahweh and Hagar, where the One with ultimate power understands/hears (*yišmaʿ*) those who are in an absolute state of powerlessness.

While the presence of Ishmael and the name itself are signs of hope, the manner in which Ishmael functions in society is problematic. This is particularly the case for those contemporary believers who hold firmly to the notion that God does not intentionally bring into being conflictual situations. Yet in 16:12, the text is certain; Ishmael will be a character of conflict. In the case of the particular relationship with Hagar, Ishmael will be able to accomplish that of which Hagar was

---

on the future son Ishmael, is presented as the only, and most effective divine response to woman's predicament. Her own physical and emotional anguish is not taken into account," "The Literary Characterization," 132.

deprived.[42] But a larger theological issue looms in 16:12, and it points to a God who indeed shapes a future that is not ideal according to human standards, and may not fit the established human norms.[43] Ishmael would come to challenge the power structure and create conflict, not only with strangers but with his own kin.

Even as Hagar fades as the focus of this encounter, her naming of the deity ushers in an extraordinary moment in the history of salvation for the marginalized. That this comes after Yahweh's pronouncement for her to return to Sarai, is all the more remarkable. Yahweh as a God who sees, not only points to the specific experience of Hagar, but serves as a point of hope for future generations of all people.[44] As she returns to Sarai, Hagar will again be voiceless and anonymous, but then she will be bearing a son, named *God hears* and believing in a God named *God sees*. The hearing and seeing by God proclaim God as a hospitable and compassionate God.[45] Even though Hagar takes a risk in returning to the status of slave, her new identity is now predicated on the belief that God sees, God hears, and God shapes the future. Hagar will indeed need the

---

42. See Trible (*Texts of Terror*, 17), who observes the parallels of "hand" and "face" in 16:12 with Hagar's words: "From the *face* of Sarai my mistress I am fleeing" (16:12), and Yahweh's words to Hagar, "Return to your mistress and suffer affliction under her *hand*" (16:12). Thus Trible concludes, "In Ishmael, Hagar's story continues."

43. Commenting on Gen 25:23 and the predicted conflict between Jacob and Esau, Brueggemann, says, "The oracle is against all conventional wisdom . . . It affirms that we do not live in a world where all possibilities are kept open and we may choose one posture as we please. It does not deny freedom. But it requires us to speak about *destiny*, about the working of this Other One who will have a voice in the future," *Genesis*, 215.

44. Croatto's words regarding the significance of the exodus event is pointedly relevant here. "The profundity does not consist in the historical phenomenon as it might be photographed or registered in a Chronicle, but in its significance, which can be understood only at a distance and which is 'said' in the Word . . . The past becomes 'promise' for those who hearken to this Word," *Exodus*, 14. Teubal, in a somewhat different vein, parallels Croatto's perspective: "In the context of the story of Hagar, the power of the 'sacred' in the text is a constant that requires renewal from generation to generation. The voice in the wilderness is female also . . . Their stories have been left to us for a purpose; so that their traditions may serve future generations," *Hagar the Egyptian*, 191.

45. See Fretheim, "The tendency in OT scholarship has been to forfeit many such metaphors . . . One needs to ask what speaking of God's eyes and ears (2 Kings 19:16) adds to the relationship of God to world that living, seeing and hearing do not. Such language makes the idea that God receives the world into himself vivid and concrete. God's experience of the world is not superficial; God takes it in, in as real a way as people do who use their eyes and ears. At the same time, in ways that people do not, God takes it *all* in (Jer. 32:19) and not with fleshly eyes (Job 10:4)," *The Suffering of God*, 9.

strength of her experience, as it is clear that, as this portion of the narrative comes to an end, the focus shifts to Abram and reestablishes Hagar as a woman in the shadows. It is Abram who is set apart in relation to Ishmael (16:11); it is Abram who does the naming (16:15). Hagar is the vehicle and to underline this role, the narrator thrice uses the phrase, "Hagar *bore* Abram." Trible, pointing to the patriarchal orientation of the narrative, observes that, "the ending undercuts Sarai [also]. The one who spoke of building up herself, not Abram, through Hagar's child receives no mention at all. Neither Hagar nor Sarai, but Abram has a son whom he names Ishmael. Among the many ironies here is the fact that the name Ishmael in no way reflects the experience of Abram, yet he does the naming. Patriarchy is well in control. The conclusion to a scene otherwise focused on women, resumes Abram's story."[46]

Protecting the Promise?

Even though the Hagar narrative typically resumes at 21:9, the preceding eight verses are instructive in casting the overall picture. As was the case in 16:15, it is established that Genesis 21 continues the story of Abram. In 21:2–5 Sarah *bears* Abraham a son (2x); Abraham names Isaac; Abraham circumcises Isaac. It is with this focus on Abraham as the promise-bearer that we come to v. 9.

It is in the context of a feast for Isaac that Sarah's fear, now stark as she imagines the future, rears its head. The text is silent regarding the birth and rearing of Ishmael. There is no implied, let alone explicit reason for Sarah's sudden action.[47] As was the case before, the focus of Sarah's comment is on Hagar as Egyptian and slave; perhaps now however, rather than an issue of esteem and power, it is a fear of the future. Sarah's tone suggests clearly that Ishmael is an unworthy heir. Even though some elements in the rabbinic tradition have sought to

---

46. Trible, *Texts of Terror*, 19.

47. The Hebrew word for what Ishmael was doing (v. 9b) is *meṣaḥeq*, from the root *ṣḥq*, precisely the same root out of which the name Isaac is borne. JoAnn Hackett suggests: "So when Ishmael is *meṣaḥēq*, he is not just laughing or playing—he is also 'Isaac-ing.' And this is perhaps what Sarah is complaining about in the next verse, that she noticed that Ishmael was doing something to indicate he was just like Isaac, that they were equals, and it is this that threatens her so," "Rehabilitating Hagar," 20–21.

create a sinister and a to-be-blamed character out of Ishmael, there is no such evidence in the text.[48]

A contemporary corollary here is the prevalent notion that it is difficult, if not impossible to have similar levels of power among classes and races and nations. Even in the midst of apparent harmony between groups of different origins and status, often either written or unwritten rules dictate behavior, levels of acceptance, and mores indicating sociocultural protocol. On an international level, some nations seek unrivaled superiority, and if challenged, there is the potential for war. In certain countries, despite legislation, distinctions are still made amongst races, distinctions that often perpetuate systemic discrimination.[49] Often, the issue is not fear of being dominated, as it is fear of equality![50]

Sarah's fear is sharp and to the point. Ishmael must go, precisely because he is perceived to be a threat to the inheritance that she believes is rightfully Isaac's (21:10).[51] It might be argued that Sarah is intolerant of anyone who would challenge Isaac, whether the threat is real or imagined.[52] On a larger scale, Sarah's words indicate what might occur

---

48. So notes Darr, *Far More Precious than Jewels*, 149. See also Tarlow and Want, "Bad Guys." The authors observe that Ishmael is portrayed by several midrashic commentators as rapist, incestuous rascal, and one who participates in "blood sports." The commentators conclude that in light of these violent characteristics, Sarah's actions are perfectly commendable (22). Suggesting that the play between Isaac and Ishmael is purely innocent, see von Rad, *Genesis*, 227; and Speiser, *Genesis*, 155.

49. India, where the caste system has been in vogue for the duration of the country's life, legislation has not eliminated the division.

50. See Trible, "Sarah, wife of Abraham, and Hagar, wife of Abraham; Sarah, woman on the pedestal, and Hagar, woman in the gutter; Sarah, mother of Isaac, and Hagar, mother of Ishmael. Potential equality between sons counters actual inequality between their mothers," "Genesis 22," 186–87.

51. Some scholars have sought to exonerate Sarah by suggesting that in fact she acted nobly on Hagar's and Ishmael's behalf. See, e.g., Sarna, "What Sarah demanded was that Hagar and her son be given their freedom thereby renouncing all claim to a share in the family estate," *Understanding Genesis*, 156. Likewise Westermann, "What Sarah is providing for is her son's future. To censure Sarah's demand from the point of view of individual ethic or our own religious attitude is to fail to see that Sarah is engaged in a struggle for her own very existence," *Genesis 12-36*, 339. Westermann's perspective creates a troublesome paradigm for those who would pursue a future based on a promise. To defend Sarah at this point, is to support a sort of biblical parochialism. A proper understanding of the promise to Abraham and Sarah, and the affection we have for the matriarch Sarah, must not hinge on defending an unjust act.

52. Soelle concludes that "Death is what takes place within us when we look upon others not as gift, blessing or stimulus, but as threat, danger, competition," *Death by Bread Alone*, 4.

when those in bondage are made free. On the other hand though, Sarah is perhaps very aware that even though Ishmael is not the son of the promise, he is nevertheless the first-born son of Abraham, and is therefore entitled. Sarah confuses the nature of the promise, which establishes Isaac as the heir, and Ishmael as the firstborn.

Could Isaac not continue to be the child of the promise if Ishmael takes his rightful place as the first-born? Under ordinary circumstances, the first-born in Israelite life occupied a distinctive place. When the legal tradition favored Sarah, she used and abused it; when the legal tradition did not serve her purposes she abandoned it.[53] Similar to 16:5, Sarah calls on Abraham to take action, except that on this occasion, the demand is very explicit and Abraham complies. Abraham's response, while sympathetic to Ishmael, is woefully lacking in care for Hagar. Indeed, even though in 16:3, Hagar is given to Abraham as a wife, that relationship is never reflected in any manner of address.[54] Abraham's distress is pin-pointed by Yahweh as having to do with Ishmael, and Yahweh's admonition makes it clear that the issue at stake is the promise, and Isaac is the one to carry on the promise.

Both Hagar and Ishmael are acceptable only as props. Indeed the decision to make a nation out of Ishmael seems to be done more as a favor to Abraham (21:13). Abraham's action in sending off Hagar and Ishmael prefigures the sacrifice of Isaac in Genesis 22. The departure (21:14) reflects the stress of the time as Abraham rises early and provides food and water for Hagar and Ishmael. The farewell is strained and distant, as Abraham watches his wife and son leave, not only his home, a place of identity for them, but his life. Again and again for the sake of the promise, parents and children will be separated (Gen 25:6). In the death of Abraham, Isaac and Ishmael will be reunited (Gen 25:9).

Hagar's existence has been a roller coaster of life and death experiences and Sarah's action to cast her out points to still another milestone of death. Not only is Hagar's departure distressing, but particularly so is her "wandering." The Hebrew *t'h* implies uncertainty with no par-

---

53. Tamez argues that "the marginalised demand as first-born sons to be included in the history of salvation. They break the order of things. They complicate history," "The Woman," 9.

54. Teubal notes that, "in Genesis 21 E depicts Hagar in the most disparaging terms. Her name is only mentioned once in v. 9, and her designation has been changed from *shifhah* to *amah*, slave. The designation of her son is equally disdainful, *ben-ha-amah*, son of the slave," *Hagar the Egyptian*, 51.

ticular destination in mind.⁵⁵ Now with a child, Hagar has no outlook for life. Any kind of wandering has an air of uncertainty and death, but wandering in the wilderness is more pointed in the direction of death. The destination in her first fleeing from Sarai was the wilderness, but in that instance it was the mark of freedom, for it was an act designed and executed by Hagar. However, in 21:14 Hagar is cast into the wilderness, and this is an act that is against her desires. Trible notes, "Departing her land of bondage, Hagar knows not exodus, but exile."⁵⁶

Moved by a Mother's Tears

When one is in exile, death comes in different ways: loss of land, community, and not least, the deep rooted questioning of the role of the divine (Lamentations 1–2). Hagar faces not only these hostile elements, but alone with her son, she faces literal death, in the reality of her son. Her "casting off" of Ishmael under one of the bushes is deafening in its portrayal of the quality of Hagar's grief. Clearly Hagar expects Ishmael to die and simply does not wish to witness it. Later, Miriam and her mother would also stand at a distance to see what would happen with Moses as he floats helplessly down the Nile. The preparation of Moses and the sight of Pharaoh's daughter's acceptance and adoption of Moses brought life to Miriam and her mother. Hagar had no such expectation. It is interesting to note that in Pharaoh's mandate to cast all the newborn boys into the Nile (Exod 1:22) as a way of eliminating the threat, the Hebrew term *tašlîkuhû* is used. This is the same verb employed by the narrator in Hagar's "casting off" (*vattašlek*) of Ishmael. The intent and expectation of death are prominent.

The poignancy of the description of Hagar is deeply affective. Trible captures Hagar's state when she says, "Her grief like her speech is sufficient unto itself. She does not cry out to another; she does not beseech God. A madonna alone with her dying child, Hagar weeps."⁵⁷

When God finally speaks to Hagar, she is addressed as one who faces an uncertain future: "Do not be afraid." This is not a generic or empty greeting but one that recognizes human fear of a future unknown.⁵⁸

---

55. See, e.g., Gen 37:15; Isa 53:16; Job 38:41.
56. Trible, *Texts of Terror*, 23.
57. Ibid., 25.
58. See, e.g., Gen 15:1, 26: 24, 46; Num 14:9; Deut 31:8; Josh 8:1; Isa 41:10; Matt 1:20; Luke 1:30, 2:10.

While it is the fear of Hagar that is addressed, it is the son to whom the attention of Yahweh is directed: (a) lift up the boy; (b) hold him fast; (c) I will make a great nation of him. It is only after these explicit directions are given that Hagar finally sees. In seeing, she finds water and then it is Ishmael's thirst that is quenched. Hagar as an oppressed and utterly marginalized woman not only fulfilled her maternal role, but fathered Ishmael.[59] Later, while Abraham would be in charge of finding a wife for Isaac, Hagar shoulders that responsibility for Ishmael (21:21).

---

59. Cf. Zipporah's role in the life of her son when Moses was absent, Exod 4:25.

2

From Particularity to Universality

Genesis 18

No matter how quickly one opens the door, no matter how generously one welcomes the stranger into one's home, no matter how disarming one's conversation is, one still has not taken the crucial step that alone would prove one's willingness to reveal one's self to the very strangeness of the stranger. For to do that one would have to do something radically different from welcoming the stranger into one's home: One would have to leave one's home and go disarmed into the territory of the stranger.[1]

Of Burning Bushes and Bright Lights

DOES GOD CONTINUE TO BE REVEALED IN THIS PRESENT AGE? AND IF so, in what form or expression? Many today find themselves troubled and confused by the inherent ambiguity of life experiences as they seek an answer to this important, pertinent question. We are readily and admittedly cognizant of the biblical references of God coming to Moses and Abraham and Sarah and Hannah, among others; but are there similar occurrences in contemporary society?

One encounters a wide range of responses to this query. There are those who adamantly claim that God is, indeed, present and active: that God, from time to time chooses people to whom God would be revealed. Included in this group are some seeking precise documentation of time and place of such revelation and naming such a revelation a

1. Miller, *The Way of Suffering*, 35.

"conversion" or a "born-again" experience. Others, while taking seriously the fact that revelation continues to occur, admit to the possibility that humans may fail to discern the event itself and/or the significance of the same. Still others remain staunchly cynical about God's willingness and/or ability of self-revelation in contemporary society under any circumstances.

So today, as indeed in generations gone by, many struggle with the perplexity and uncertainty of the event, nature and significance of the revelation of God to and through humanity.[2]

While I have not personally known of anyone who has had a literal burning bush experience recently or has been blinded by a light on any road, such a lack of a specific encounter offers less than sufficient evidence that God no longer reveals God's self. Rather, it seems to me, one must seek biblical warrant in an attempt to discover God's revelation in common, everyday-life events, as well as in traditional patterns of revelation.

While the messianic event for the Christian is the event that brings salvation, one would boldly assert that this is not the final event in which the intent of God is revealed.[3] In a variety of circumstances, divine revelation continues. Were we to believe that revelation has ceased, we would, in actuality, place blinders on God, effectively seeking to restrict God. How will God be revealed, and to whom and for what purpose? The answers to these questions remain part of the surprise that God brings to the partnership that God offers to humanity.

In both the Hebrew Bible and New Testament, we hear of countless instances where the acts and words of God are revealed in ways that stun both the recipients and the witnesses: Jonah, who would try to escape the call to bring a good word to the Ninevites (Jon 1:3); members of the religious establishment who would seek to stop those who were hungry from harvesting grain on the Sabbath (Mark 2:23–28). In these

---

2. See Jung, *Memories, Dreams, Reflections*, who speaks of discerning the "will of God." In this connection he points to the complexity of the matter and the danger of speaking in absolutes about the meaning of the revelations of God.

3. See Martinson, "The Crucified and Risen Buddha?" Martinson makes an important distinction between salvation and revelation and in the process suggests that revelation is "infinitely repeatable. Salvation on the other hand, is first of all an event independent of any subjective situation and as such is once-for-all and unrepeatable—the people of Israel once rescued from Egypt are rescued, and this is so regardless of how they feel about it or whether they even know it or not," 227.

examples we have instances that have not only remained dynamic in their original context, but have created for others of all time a life-giving framework in which to function.

To be sure, these difficult expressions of grace could more easily be left within the historical framework. Yet, the reality is that, surely, we must pursue ways of inquiry and examination by which we might begin to understand the nature and manner of God's revelation in the here and now.

Levels of Hospitality

The Genesis text before us is one that is well known, so much so that often there is a tendency to overlook some of the sharp, unsettling, complex elements in it. Surely in this text we have a concrete idea of one response that might call for living a righteous and just life. How do we know God is revealed today? As we explore this text, there are three levels of hospitality that surface.

First, there is the literal hospitality that is meted out to the strangers who come to the door of Abraham and Sarah's tent. On one level, this might appear to be a reflection of eastern hospitality and nothing more: the culture virtually required such hospitality of Abraham and Sarah and such an event had no extraordinary dimensions. However, this study will attempt to show that what Abraham and Sarah offered to these strangers was significantly more than mere requirement. Hospitality executed bridges the chasm between centrality and marginality.

Second, there is an emphasis in this text on newness and transformation. The act of hospitality is intrinsically tied to the promise and gift of newness. God's purpose in creating any and all aspects of creation bears an inherent expectation that each aspect of creation must be willing to be a gift to all other aspects of creation--hospitality to others is most definitely one expression of giftedness for creation.

Third, the gift of hospitality comes alive also in the second half of this text. While this is more of a metaphorical understanding, the reality is that both God and Abraham seek to bring life and grace to a people who are not only undeserving, but appear bent on self-destruction.

Typically, the focus of these stories have zeroed in on the laughter of Sarah and the destruction of Sodom. The reality is that Sarah did laugh, and Sodom was destroyed. But as interesting as these might be, they are hardly the central points of the story. One does necessarily question the historicity of the laughter or the act of destruction, but perhaps what is necessary here is a decentralizing of these events and the discerning of new and more valid centralities, centralities which might be shaped by issues of marginality. Part of the essential challenge of biblical study is to engage with the material in an imaginative manner. The personalities and themes that have been couched comfortable at the center by tradition, and have remained there for centuries must be examined again. Our eyes must not be closed by the possibility of realignment of the central and marginal.

Imagining the Future

A re-reading of this text, with an eye for detail and the unexpected allows the narrative to burst forth into the realm of imagination and wonder. In a macrocosmic framework, these stories paint a picture of grace and hospitality on the part of many who are sometimes the recipients and sometimes the source of the gift.

Before we hear the response of Sarah or see the destruction of Sodom, we experience demonstrations of hospitality and grace. Disbelief and destruction are not the primary focus of the narrator. If, indeed, as we have so often done, we remain in the scenes of laughter and destruction the intended portrayal of the narrator escapes us.

Moreover, using this text as a metaphor for a larger canvas, one might say that remaining at the point of destruction is to remain in the present setting of reality. To see the present as the end is to miss the essence of the gospel: the unfolding future which may hold unexpected surprises, offering risk, challenge, delight and blessing. Our myopic human expectations assume that the present reality also defines the shape of the future: nothing will change.

The Hebrew Bible is replete with instances where elements of newness and grace push the characters in the narrative back to significant points of origin: in the fleeing of Elijah from the clutches of Ahab and Jezebel, Elijah would return to Sinai and seek the counsel of God (1 Kings 19); Hosea in pointing to the elements of newness and grace, has Yahweh returning, with Israel, to the scene of the wilderness for a new beginning (Hosea 2). Here, the setting is Mamre, a setting with important connections for Abraham and Sarah. This is the place where Abraham built an altar to Yahweh immediately after receiving the promise of the land (Gen 13:18).

Throughout Israelite history, the building of an altar particularized the presence of God in the midst of the life experiences of the people; thus the attention of the reader is directed beyond the singularity of a place for worship. The presence of an altar at Mamre designated this location as something of a holy shrine. This building of altars directs the attention of readers beyond having a place of worship, for it surely points to the ongoing presence of God in all the circumstances of the peoples' lives. Within this context, Abraham again encounters God. Worship is not the focus here, but rather the important connection between human beings and Yahweh. In this setting, we find important implications for our understanding of the expectations of God in the lives of the people.

Urgency of Hospitality

In the midst of their journey, a journey led by Yahweh, a journey with an unknown destination, Abraham, Sarah and their entourage make a temporary stop at Mamre. Within the context of being sojourners and travelers themselves, Abraham and Sarah are visited by three traveling strangers. Though they are tenting, and not at an established place of residence, Abraham and Sarah become the ones who would provide for these strangers. The hospitality offered, thus, is borne neither from wealth nor power.[4] Such a demonstration of person-to-person hospitality allows one to view Mamre as a representation of the presence of God in the midst of life, at any given point along the journey.

The story unfolds in "the heat of the day," a time when it is uncomfortable to be out-doors, especially if one is traveling.[5] Even God rec-

---

4. See Breech, *Jesus and Postmodernism*, 44, who notes that, "The idea of providing hospitality to travelers was deeply ingrained in the ancient world and, in some of the stories and myths, we find the notion that there would be a divine reward or a divine punishment, depending on whether one helped travelers in need of assistance. Breech also notes that classical material such as the *Odyssey* testify to the importance of hospitality, the absence of which might very well lead to tragedy. The parallels to which he alludes, between the Abraham narrative and Ovid (89 n. 49), underline the fact that the "stranger" might be a god in disguise, hence, a greater incentive for acting hospitably (cf. Heb 13:20). While this might be true, one does not wish to establish this as the reason for Abraham's actions.

5. Cf. Gen 3:8, where it is a pleasant time of day for taking a walk outdoors.

ognizes the importance of having a shade in the midst of the heat of the day (cf. Jon 4:6). Typically, one is at rest during the "heat of the day"; Abraham and Sarah might have been justified in remaining indoors and disregarding the arrival of these visitors. But to have done so would have been to neglect the travelers in their weariest state of being and overlook their state of powerlessness. Hunger, thirst, weariness and heat, here and elsewhere in Genesis, all contribute to human vulnerability (Gen 25:29–34). Abraham understandably is indoors but he sees the strangers and goes out to greet them. We have a glimpse of the importance that Abraham attaches to this act.

Abraham's gestures of greeting and receiving the guests constitute a statement that they have been made a part of the community. Moreover, at this juncture, Abraham's actions point to his own confidence in his particular journey.[6] In today's society, even as we greet invited friends or relatives, the element of welcoming is inherent in the definition of hospitality. What, then, of uninvited visitors? Are we now in a category that challenges our own present reality? Do we ignore the challenge to move from words to actions? To have remained unwelcome would reflect the brokenness within society. The sharing of an extravagant meal with the visitors offers a place of belonging. Van Seters is aware of this when he concludes that, "this is certainly more than a show of politeness."[7]

The extravagance of Abraham is exhibited not simply by the quantity of food prepared and offered.[8] Throughout the text, there is a sense of urgency in Abraham's actions. First, Abraham runs (v. 2) to the door to meet the strangers; he then hastens (v. 6) into the tent to tell Sarah; on the heels of this he runs (v. 7) to find an appropriate calf for the meal and finally we are told that the servants hasten (v. 7) to prepare it. It is clear that there is an overarching element of urgency here.[9] The concern

---

6. See Nouwen, *The Wounded Healer*, 92: "One who has come to terms with his own loneliness and is at home in his house is a host who offers hospitality to his guests. He gives them a friendly space, where they may feel free to come and go, to be close and distant, to rest and to play, to talk and to be silent, to eat and to fast. The paradox indeed is that hospitality asks for the creation of any empty space where the guest can find his own soul."

7. Van Seters, *Abraham in History and Tradition*, 212.

8. See Breech, *The Silence of Jesus*, 88ff., who notes that three measures of meal is over sixty pounds of flour, enough to feed over a hundred people. This is what Abraham produced after he invites the guests to a "morsel of bread!"

9. See Brueggemann, "'Impossibility' and Epistemology," 617, who notes that "In vv. 2–8, the verbal pattern which warrants attention is the cluster of verbs related to *haste*

for the welfare of the strangers propels him to disregard the heat of the day and proceed with haste in order to take care of the needs of these uninvited guests.

Moreover, Abraham, from his initial contact with the strangers, positions himself as the one who would serve. The one called by Yahweh to lead, herein is also called to serve, and does so with extravagant hospitality. Jesus manifests the ultimate expression of this tension of one who is called to lead and responds with unprecedented service. In the face of his suffering and crucifixion he would in fact take time to care for, and show hospitality to those in his midst, even a stranger on a cross.[10]

Identity Unknown

There is no indication in this text that Abraham is aware of the identity of any of the strangers. While the narrator begins the story by telling the readers that Yahweh appeared to Abraham, Abraham's verbal greeting clues us to the fact that he is totally unaware of the identity of the strangers. In part this is established through his use of the generic Hebrew term ʾ*adonai*, translated, "lord." This generic term of respect intrinsically connects to Abraham's manner of bowing himself to the earth. Such an intentional mode of servanthood moves beyond curtsy and genuflection. Both the bowing and the greeting of "my lord" create a hospitable environment and the strangers are able to respond appropriately. By his actions, Abraham portrays one who not only acts hospitably, but is likewise the recipient of kindness. Though the reward for Abraham's hospitality is not articulated, nor constitutes the motivation for his actions, the reciprocity factors into the larger picture of the full definition of hospitality.[11] In this regard, one only has to reflect on the words of Jesus in Luke 19:1–27.

The reward in the case of Abraham is not spelled out and is surely not the motivation for his act. Using a stunningly simple agrarian met-

---

(*ruṣ, mahar*) . . . The sequence of five verbs—*ruṣ/mahar/mahar/ruṣ/mahar/*—creates the mood for this part of the narrative. Abraham and his two aides (Sarah and the servants) are all in haste."

10. See Luke 22:50ff. and the incident regarding the restoration of the soldier's ear.

11. Van Seters posits the theory that hospitality leads to reward and inhospitality to destruction. *Abraham in History and Tradition*, 211. As interesting as this dichotomy is, in its simplicity it has misapprehended the complexity of the theologian's design. On the connection between hospitality and reciprocity, see Herzfeld, "'As in your House.'"

aphor, Jerome Miller underlines the importance of the unencumbered nature of hospitality: "in my very manner of hoeing I am open to the earth itself, irrespective of its yielding or not yielding me any practical benefits; when I am open to the hoe itself not just as a tool but as a being which deserves my attention in its own right; and when I am open to the very act of hoeing, not just as a means to a goal but as the interplay of hand, hoe and earth."[12] Hospitality is a privilege. The reward to himself occurs in the willingness of the strangers to allow him to be their gracious host. The radicality of this mode of thinking is seen in part by the thorough departure from the common mode of hospitality. As much as the strangers are hungry and hot, their dignity is maintained as mutuality is established. We would recall also that Abraham's promise for the future includes at its core the call to be a blessing to others, regardless of their religious, social, economic or ethnic identity (Gen 12:3). Similar responsibility would be central to any call where the promise-maker is God.[13]

There is an intrinsic connection between the one who gives and the one who receives.[14] At this point Abraham is the one who has been gifted with food. His property of cattle and other assets have come in part as gifts from others who were themselves strangers, as is the case in the encounter with Abimelech (Gen 20:14-16; cf. 13:2). Here too, the wealth of Abraham did not come entirely from his personal toil, but indeed from the consequences of actions that were contrary to what God had planned (Gen 12:10-20; 20:14ff.). Even under these circumstances,

---

12. Miller, *The Way of Suffering*, p. 24.

13. Brueggemann, *Genesis*, 131, observes that the "common economic view in which modern persons are schooled, capitalists and Marxists alike, is *scarcity*. Social policy, personal conduct and international politics are conducted on a presupposition of scarcity . . . The matter of dividing up the wealth is a place at which the power of the promise and the ideology of scarcity come into urgent conflict." The hospitality of Abraham and his household overcomes this conflict and establishes a paradigm for resolving this sort of conflict in other arena.

14. See Stegner, *Narrative Theology in Early Jewish Christianity*, 71. Stegner notes the interplay of word between Genesis 18 and Exodus 16. In so doing he suggests that God rewards Abraham's hospitality. He quotes Bertil Gärtner as saying, "Thus what Abraham did for God, God did for the children of Israel in the desert. Abraham brought water, and so God gave water to the people to drink through the rock in the desert. Abraham served bread, and the people received manna, bread from heaven. Abraham escorted 'the three men' down toward Sodom, and so God went with the people in the pillars of fire and cloud."

Abraham would be the beneficiary. Here too, the benefit to Abraham despite his own brokenness would be a basis for the importance of being hospitable. As was the case throughout their journey to the land which God promised them, we come to see that both Abraham and Sarah would be granted acts of grace even when they were undeserving.

Often on the surface Abraham clearly was the one to blame for not trusting God to lead. Yet, acts of grace would remind him and us that this God is one who will lead the people in all circumstances even when they have taken matters into their own hands and have faltered. The reality is that the call of Abraham and Sarah is not predicated on their deserving or their directing. If anything the act of grace reflected in their call, is one that catapults them out of a dead-end reality into a future, which though uncertain, directs them to a new life. So too, the reception of the strangers by Abraham and Sarah is not predicated on the strangers' identity, but on the basis of their present reality which was one of hunger, thirst and fatigue.

Though we are not told of the nationality of the strangers, the nature of hospitality demands that care is to be granted to all people without the knowledge of any intrinsic belonging. In the matter of hospitality, issues such as ethnicity, nationality, religious affiliation, political ideology and socio-economic status have no place. As Miller observes, "Hospitality is a rupture of boundaries. It involves welcoming as friend the Other whom I experience as stranger. But I can experience the Other as stranger only if I experience him as *Other*, different, independent, approaching me across a frontier which separates us."[15] The ministry of Jesus is a positive patchwork of occasions where he dons the role of stranger as he enters the lives of the people. It is not surprising therefore that it is the stranger which is singled out as a paradigm for the nature of the believer's presence in the world.[16] One is further reminded of the situa-

---

15. Miller, *The Way of Suffering*, 25.

16. See Palmer, *The Company of Strangers*, 22–23, who is surely right when he concludes: "The God who cares about our private lives is concerned with our public lives as well. This is a God who calls us into relationship not only with family and friends, but with strangers scattered across the face of the earth, a God who says again and again, 'we are in this together' . . . The church preaches a vision of human unity which means very little if not acted out in the public realm. Surely that vision applies to more than family and friends. Surely it is a vision which claims more than the commonality of those who think and act and look alike. Surely that vision reaches out to include those who are alien, different, strange. If so, then the church *must* incarnate its vision in public, for there and only there is the stranger to be found."

tion between Moses and the daughters of Jethro at the well. To be sure Moses shows hospitality to the women in his help against the shepherds, and equally important is the fact that Jethro in welcoming Moses, does not establish his care on the latter's identity. Indeed Moses is introduced as an Egyptian: the reality therefore is that Moses was an outsider (Exod 2:16–22).

Hospitality and Servanthood

The biblical idea of footwashing is hinted at here, though the text does not specifically state that Abraham washes the feet of the visitors. Nevertheless it adds to the expression of servanthood. Again, Jesus as the one who washes the feet of the disciples is the ultimate paradigm of what it means to be a servant. Despite Peter's obduracy, Jesus makes clear the centrality of servanthood in the framework of what it means to follow Christ. "For I have given you an example, that you also should do as I have done to you" (John 13:15). If one would be a bearer of the gospel or be a promise bearer as Abraham and Sarah were, then they would have to be servants. In effect Jesus takes an issue such as footwashing, traditionally reserved for the marginalized and transposes it to a place of centrality. Those who seek to function at the center must do so with a new reality of what is central and what is marginal.

From the moment of greeting the strangers, one hears the 'no strings attached' attitude in the words and acts of welcome. In contemporary society, one often hears an implication of 'strings attached' and expectations formed, if, and when one offers hospitality to another.[17] The biblical reality is that the equality of the one receiving an hospitable act is never up for negotiation. The requirement of hospitality is based on the right of every human being to shape his/her life in accordance with being in the *imago dei*.[18]

---

17. Nouwen, *The Wounded Healer*, 89, concludes that, "it has become very difficult for us today to fully understand the implication of hospitality. Like the Semitic nomads, we live in a desert with many lonely travelers who are looking for a moment of peace, for a fresh drink and for a sign of encouragement so that they can continue their mysterious search for freedom."

18. See Weil, *Waiting for God*, 139. Addressing the connection between justice and charity Weil observes, "if the gift is rightly given and rightly received, the passing of a morsel of bread from one man to another is something like a real communion. Christ does not call his benefactors loving or charitable. He calls them just. The Gospel makes

Wiesel maintains that the "other" cannot be treated as a stranger, an outsider in a value neutral manner, for if this happens, then death is the inevitable consequence. Moreover, Wiesel notes that the notion of the stranger brings suspicion, and suspicion leads to death.[19] Abraham in his open and urgent attention to the visitors, ensures that there are no barriers and removes whatever mutual suspicion there might be. In two different ways, the words of Wiesel apply here. In a metaphorical sense the continued treatment of the visitors in a distant manner would have led to a certain death in terms of the clinical atmosphere. Then of course, if Abraham did not provide the food and drink, perhaps the visitors might literally have died.

Abraham is not only gracious in his reception, but there is a sense of urgency. He is attentive to the fact that the strangers have a journey of their own. Like Abraham and Sarah, the travelers have to continue on their journey. To this end, Abraham tells the visitors that he recognizes the need to move on and hence the haste (v. 5). To be sure they have the freedom to stay, but in the framework of hospitality, one who gives must recognize the human journey of the other. That is but a fundamental right of the recipient.

Particularity to Universality

The particularity of the strangers' journey serves as a metaphor for understanding an important component in the journey motif. While all

---

no distinction between the love of our neighbor and justice . . . Our notion of justice dispenses him who possesses from the obligation of giving."

19. Wiesel interview with Bill Moyers. See also Ogletree, *Hospitality to the Stranger*, 2–3, who suggests that, "To offer hospitality to a stranger is to welcome something new, unfamiliar, and unknown into our life-world. On the one hand, hospitality requires a recognition of the stranger's vulnerability in an alien social world. Strangers need shelter and sustenance in their travels, especially when they are moving through a hostile environment. On the other hand, hospitality designates occasions of potential discovery which can open up our narrow provincial world . . . The stranger does not simply challenge or subvert our assumed world of meaning; she may enrich, even transform, that world.

"In its metaphorical usage, hospitality does not refer simply to literal instances of interactions with persons from societies and cultures other than our own. It suggests attention to "otherness" in its many expressions: wonder and awe in the presence of the holy, receptivity to unconscious impulses arising from our being as bodied selves, openness to the unfamiliar and unexpected in our most intimate relationships . . ."

journeys perhaps share certain common ingredients, each journey taken has a distinct character and is shaped by particular circumstances.

As we continue through the text, the reference to food is captured in the synecdocal statement, "morsel of bread." It is not so much a matter of modesty on the part of Abraham, but rather "morsel of bread" points to all that is necessary for daily sustenance.[20] In this regard, it parallels the petition in the Lord's prayer. "Our daily bread" emphasizes the need for physical sustenance and even as Jesus prayed to God for this element of life, there is the implicit reminder that this is for all people. Soelle captures succinctly the importance of bread and the manner in which it encapsulates one component of the relation between the human being and God: "bread, the fruit of human labor, is a sign of God's grace."[21] All people need physical sustenance and it is an inherent expectation that it will be granted.

What Abraham does is to take the expectation to a prodigious limit and this is naturally expressed in both the quality and the quantity of the food. The abundance of cakes and the quality of meat ("tender and good" calf) underline the extravagant reception. Hospitality and sustenance are therefore not defined by doing the bare minimum, but rather expressing the kind of grace that God has shown and intends for all people. To be sure the grace of God can even be expressed through limited and narrow human participation (such as Jonah going only partly into the city of Nineveh, and then in a sentence pronouncing judgment rather than calling to repentance (John 3:3–4). Yet, the presence of such scarcity and meagerness of grace spell out the emphasis on grace found in this Genesis narrative.[22]

Bread represents the universal satiety for hunger, and the inclusion of the idea of feeding the guests moves this text out of the localized situation in the life of Abraham, to one which has universal implications.

20. See Bal, *Death and Dissymmetry*, 104–5. On the matter of Abraham's use of bread as an understatement, Bal discusses a literary function of the word.

21. Soelle, *To Work and to Love*, 143.

22. See Soelle, *Thinking About God*, 79. Regarding the notion of "grace," Soelle says, "grace is not just a counterpart to sin in the moral sense of the word; grace is more than acquittal before the judge... Unexpected, beyond our control, undeserved—these adjectives appear in the theological description of grace." According to Soelle, when human beings receive God's grace, it is as if "roses begin to bloom in the middle of winter" (ibid.). Grace, in other words, not only has a miraculous overtone, but there is notably the element of newness.

This reference must be understood in both particular and universal contexts, indeed, in the light of those who hunger in far away lands or locally. Children and adults die each day because of the lack of basic needs. The reality is that while we might not think that we are even remotely involved in the demise of part of creation in the form of hunger and its consequences of death, we are only deceiving ourselves when we refuse to take our full responsibility for this tragedy. Tons and tons of food are left unused in certain nations, including our own, as more than enough food is grown to feed all the peoples of the world; we fail in just and equitable distribution. How is it that we are able to wash our hands of the matter and claim that the responsibility is not ours? The death of others for want of food leaves us with blood-stained hands. As we pursue our own goals, others have been crushed indirectly, as well as intentionally—and the blood stains are the same, in either case. There are many just and appropriate reasons to wash our hands. We are instilled with this type of propriety from early on in our lives. No, we are not to wash like Pilate so that the truth might be subsumed and we be exonerated, and thus satisfy the masses for the lack of courage to do the right and just thing. Indeed, we are not even to be like Lady Macbeth who desperately seeks to cleanse her hands of blood so that she might rid herself of guilt; guilt which she harbors for shedding the blood of the innocent in order to fulfill her personal dreams. Rather, bloodstained hands must be washed in order that relationships might be restored.[23]

Kosuke Koyama says that we need to move from hostility to hospitality. Part of the reason we are hostile, even in passive ways, stems from our fear of the unfamiliar. We are afraid of the stranger. Yet, it is more than unfamiliarity, which creates this estrangement. Rather, the stranger is moreso one who is perceived to be different from us. If we do not feel at home with a person, an event etc., we often deem it strange. "We must move from hostility to hospitality. We must move from the familiar to the unfamiliar. There is no other way today. Only in this movement is there hope for the survival of humankind."[24]

---

23. See the poignant scene where Lady Macbeth longs for the blood stains to be removed from her hands (*Macbeth*, act V, scene 1) Also, note the prophet Isaiah's scorching indictment in Isa 1:10–17, especially v. 15.

24. Koyama, *Three Mile an Hour God*, 75.

Newness and Transformation

> I will surely return to you in the Spring (v. 10)
> Sarah your wife shall have a son (v. 10)
> Sarah listened . . . Sarah laughed (vv. 10–12)
>
> I will return to you in the Spring (v. 14)
> Sarah shall have a son (v. 14)
> Sarah denied . . . "I did not laugh" (v. 15).

As we have seen, hospitality includes both giving and receiving. This section of the narrative alerts us to an additional factor inherent in hospitality: that of promise. Yahweh promises Sarah and Abraham that he would return to them in the Spring. This promise, not given prior to the hospitable acts of Abraham and Sarah, comes on the heels of the strangers having eaten and rested, as a surprise to both of them.

Neither Abraham nor Sarah had any reason to expect a progeny given their age situation and the barrenness of Sarah, much less, that a promise of this nature would come from these transient visitors. While Sarah laughs, this is as much an act of disbelief as the silence of Abraham.[25] Indeed, for all practical purposes, for the remainder of this discussion of Yahweh's return in the spring, Abraham is not an active participant. The structure of vv. 10–15 points to the promise given and the reassurance made by God. Moreover, there is the subtle literary shift in the narrative from the conversation with Abraham to an indirect, and finally to a direct discourse with Sarah. One of the ongoing questions here is whether Abraham and Sarah are able to believe that Yahweh is capable of moving beyond death to life.[26] In the case of this couple, death took the form of barrenness.[27]

The text does not tell us that either Abraham or Sarah had any reason to recognize the stranger to be Yahweh. The text *does* tell us of transformation in the form of the promise of an heir. This encounter with Yahweh results in radical transformation—encounter with God always results in transformation. While numerous examples in the

---

25. See Breech, *The Silence of Jesus*, 96, who observes that while laughter is a very complex phenomenon, it is profoundly human.

26. See Buechner, *Peculiar Treasures*, 153. The author, in reflecting on this question, concludes: "it suddenly dawned on [Abraham and Sarah] that the wildest dreams they'd ever had hadn't been half wild enough."

27. For an excellent discussion of "barrenness" as a metaphor of death, see Brueggemann, *Genesis*, 114–26. See also Gossai, *Abraham, Sarah, and the Journey of Faith*.

biblical material underline this truth, Job and Jacob represent two paradigms of encounter.

On the surface, there is little that we might find to link these two stories, yet, undeniably, both speak uniquely of a meeting with God. For Jacob, subsequent to the encounter, transformation would result in a radical shift for him, not only in the direction of his life, but in the relationship with Esau (e.g., Gen 28:10–20; 32:22–32). In the case of Job, while he is described by God as a blameless and upright person, the narrative tells of a new encounter with God, unlike any previous relationship that Job had with God, and Job would never again be the same person. Job encounters God in a new and different way and as a result was transformed (Job 42:5). Like Job, encounters with, and faith in God were not new experiences for Abraham and Sarah, yet this specific encounter would lead them along paths not yet taken on their journey with this transformational, encounterable God.

In the pronouncement of the promise that is encapsulated in vv. 9–15, we have the reminder that God will "return" in the Spring. Twice in these verses is God's return mentioned. One does not want to stretch the meaning of this term outside of reasonable application, though one is nevertheless prompted to note that the Hebrew term used here is *shûb*. While *shûb* is literally translated "return," we must not overlook the meaning that is most often attributed to this term in the Old Testament, namely "repentance." The text under review here does not suggest that God will "repent" in the Spring, though it does imply that the return of God will indeed usher in a transformation. To be sure this will be a transformation of Abraham and Sarah and the generations that will follow them, but in a profound way this is also a hint of the relationship which is about to be established between God and a people not yet called into being.

For God, this will be a point of radical transformation as God again brings into being something that is radically new. Jeansonne reminds us that the precise wording in the Hebrew text is, *ka'eth ḥayah*, which translates as the "time when it is reviving."[28] Moreover, the "return" of God places God in a vulnerable situation as God will publicly

---

28. Jeansonne, *The Women of Genesis*, 23, who notes that the only other place where this phrase is found is in 2 Kgs 4:16, 17, which refer to the Shunnamite woman, who, like Sarah has an elderly husband and is promised that "the time when it is reviving" will be her time.

enter into partnership with a barren couple. Inasmuch as God is the promise-maker and hence the only one who will finally be able to fulfill the promise, it cannot be overstated that this is a vulnerable position for God, for surely if nothing else, God begins at a point of weakness and powerlessness. To call God vulnerable is not so much to conclude that God is weak or powerless, as it is a reflection of God's integrity. This description of the nature of God takes seriously God's alignment with humanity in a way that does not in any way reduce the freedom of the human being to be human, even in the face of God.

The promise that is given is one that moves both Abraham and Sarah out of the present reality to a future that neither of them was able to imagine. Intrinsic to the matter of newness is the ability of the recipient to believe in a word which seems to go against all odds. Neither Abraham nor Sarah could believe that a son could be born to them.[29] With the passing of the years, Abraham and Sarah must have ceased contemplating the likelihood of having a child, for their very age place such a hope in the category of the impossible. However, the issue here is much larger than that of desiring an heir. Is one able to believe in a promise that departs radically from the present and opens a future, hitherto unthinkable? Is one able to envision a future that is so out of the ordinary that it borders on the unimaginable?

In the case of Sarah, there is a four-part reaction to the announcement of the promise. Sarah listened, she laughed, she denied and she argued with God. Yet within all of these reactions by Sarah, one is never led to believe that Sarah was unwilling to proceed with the promise. Sarah, by her own actions, in no way demonstrates that this promise of God is even conceivable to her; yet, when confronted by God, she is unwilling to admit her disbelief. But God is not willing to allow the restrictive norms of human community coupled with the inability to imagine to stand in the way of the promise. Indeed, there would be the announcement of the promise and then there is the word of assurance. Yahweh's words to Sarah, "...but you did laugh" serve as a reminder that Yahweh is fully aware of all that is happening in the mind of Sarah and Yahweh is unwilling to have this inconceivability and disbelief stand in the way of the gift of newness.[30] Perhaps as important in this encounter

---

29. On this matter of bringing into being that which is perceived to be impossible, see Weil, *Waiting for God*, 149.

30. Brisman draws our attention to the presence of the Hebrew *beqirbah* in this text

between Yahweh and Sarah is a reminder that Yahweh calls us to be honest--with ourselves and with God!

God offers the gift of newness, and as one might have predicted, human inconceivability manifests itself in disbelief. The reality is that humans are unwilling and/or unable to trust the newness which God promises and authors, particularly when it takes us out of our range of human imagination. For the particular lives of Abraham and Sarah, this gift of newness would bring about a radical transformation. An even greater effect is brought on the community who, in the generations to come, will live this moment in immeasurable ways. The act of hospitality is not a static, impersonal act; it is an investment in the future, often with a scope and range beyond human imagination.

We must note here that there is no element of coercion on the part of Yahweh. On the one hand, while God would seek to grant promises to the people, it is inconsistent with God's intent and orientation to force anyone to accept these promises against his/her will. Even with Abraham and Sarah, there is no divine imposition of a decree. Given the freedom of the human being to make decisions in the face of Yahweh's promises, we must at least believe that Abraham and Sarah could have said "no" to the promise of a son for all the reasons apparent to us today. Or for that matter, Abraham could have neglected to attend to the strangers when they came to his tent. As interesting as these elements might be however, they clearly bypass the intentionality of the narrator.

This particular narrative segment portrays Abraham and Sarah as expecting no miracles. The manner in which life is disposed in the present has sealed the pattern for the future. In this regard, we might again look to the words of Koyama (above) as imploring us to move away from the familiar present into the unknown future. Though that future looms fearful in its unfamiliarity and risk, one must not dismiss the simultaneous great potential for hope. This is a future over which humanity will have little or no control. It is a future based on promise and fulfilled by the promise-maker.

---

and proposes a novel reading. "When Sarah laughs *beqirbah* (internally, in her womb, "to herself" as we more idiomatically say), Yava shows that he dwells in her midst, hears her inner laugh and ordains the reformation of that inner word into the flesh of Isaac, the Laugh within the womb." *The Voice of Jacob*, 45. While *qereb* is not conventionally used in the Old Testament to mean "womb," the connotation is clearly inherent in the term. See, e.g., Gen 25:22.

If we were to take this section of the narrative and move with it into today's community with all the realities confronting and shaping us, we would be startled by the relevant implications for our lives. For those of us living lives of comfort and complacency, containing elements of security and power, this text has the potential to be troublesome, for it calls us out of our comfort zone and seeks to open to us a new future, with all the fears and unfamiliar elements. Often, we would choose to avoid such a future. To remain where we are in security might very well lead one to arrogant complacency. Power and security have the potential to bring about arrogance. When arrogance rules a person's life, there is no anticipation, let alone eagerness for a future that may bring about change. We seek to become controllers of our own destiny, in which there is no desire for a dynamic future. Indeed, a future that is promised by God with varying degrees of newness becomes an unwelcome gift. At the other end of the spectrum are those who live with hunger and injustice and oppression as their constant companions. Here too, there is an inclination towards believing in the status quo of the situation. This is equally problematic. What both of these positions have in common is the belief that the present represents the pattern for the future. In other words there is no chance for newness. To station ourselves permanently in the present is to choose death![31]

In presenting this gift to Abraham and Sarah, God makes clear to all people that the present is never to be assumed to be the final shape of the world. Moreover, God's promise which comes to us will not allow death to have the last word, for out of death will come life. That is the element of grace that is coupled with hospitality in this text.

The second half of Genesis 18 has traditionally been separated from the preceding unit. While on the surface, the reasons for such separation might appear to be obvious, a closer look reveals a potential for an interpretation of integration as one explores the larger text. This

---

31. See Hall, *The Stewardship of Life in the Kingdom of Death*, 56. In addressing the question of stewardship, he alerts us to the importance of change from our present reality if there is going to be any chance for life: "In spite of ourselves, we find that we have to stand against our governments, against technological and economic structures, against trends and policies and values that are deeply embedded in our way of life." See also, Tillich. *Theology of Culture*, 208, who speaks of a *new reality* that pushes us to come face to face with all of the anxieties of life and still be able to come to grips with this newness. To be suffocated by anxiety and fear is to die; to take a risk and participate in this new reality opens the future and brings new life.

chapter cannot be interpreted entirely on a thematic basis, for surely the text must be considered on its own merit. However, one cannot miss what I consider to be an intrinsic connection between this unit and the preceding one.

Settings and actions change, yet Yahweh and Abraham remain the central characters. Additionally the original commission of Abraham included the blessing and care of all nations. Now Sodom becomes the direct object of such blessing and care. In the ensuing discourse (vv. 22-32) Yahweh places in a sharper focus the important elements of Abraham's journey.

Expectations of the Partnership

In vv. 16–21, the narrator introduces us to certain tensions within the heart of Yahweh, hitherto unrecognized in the narrative, namely that the relationship established between Yahweh, Abraham and Sarah included specific expectations. While Abraham and Sarah are the ones selected by Yahweh to become the cornerstone of the promise, they are not intended to be, nor do they choose to be passive participants. As they play out their role, they must respond to the call for trust and confidence in Yahweh's leadership. There will be a system of continual communication between Yahweh and Abraham and Sarah. There is an underlying understanding that when any of the three partners act outside of the boundaries of the relationship, there would be a time of reckoning. Alleviating this problem necessitates that they remain in each other's confidence and trust.

In v. 16, we have a structural transition. The visitors who had eaten and rested decide to move on. To complete the act of hospitality, Abraham walks the strangers to the place where they would resume their journey. While Abraham is doing this, there is something extraordinary transpiring. We see and hear God engaged in a mental monologue. In this, God reflects the commitment that God made with Abraham with regard to the promise. We must take careful, intentional note of four vital, interrelated components in these six verses.

First, in vv. 17-18, the narrator specifies that God takes seriously the aspect of partnership with Abraham. One might say that the actualization of newness depends on the active participation of both humans and God. This is an important expression of the human and the divine as co-creators. God feels personally responsible for the health of the partnership and acknowledges the importance of validating Abraham's role, even when Abraham may not agree with God. Fretheim notes that, "When God makes a decision, God is open to changing it in light of the ongoing conversation with the leadership of the community of faith."[32] With this in mind God wonders about the role of Abraham in light of the impending destruction that is about to befall Sodom. In the soliloquy of God, it is noted that in order for Abraham to live with the promise entrusted to him, God cannot have secrets that will finally be detrimental to Abraham and Sarah's ability to pursue fully the journey of the promise (cf. Amos 3:7).

Second, Abraham's role is inextricably tied to the promise that he will be a blessing to nations (Gen 12:3). In a way this is put to the test in this text. One of the noteworthy factors here is that Abraham is not a resident of Sodom. The discourse which takes place between Yahweh and Abraham centers around a nation which is not a direct part of the life of Abraham, except for the knowledge that Lot, his nephew resides there. If Abraham will be a blessing to other nations, then the least that must happen with Sodom is that Abraham must be allowed to demonstrate the blessing component of his commission. Abraham advocates and speaks on behalf of the voiceless innocent.

Third, for the first time in the Abraham narrative, God pinpoints the cardinal cornerstones necessary for a relationship with God: Abraham and all those who follow would have to live in justice and righteousness. While these terms are not spelled out with specifics, we know that they are the precise opposite of all that is evil and unjust in society (e.g., Amos 5:21–24, 6:12; Isa 1:10–17; 5:1–8, all of which give precise dimension to

---

32. See Fretheim. *The Suffering of God*, 51. Also, Heyward, *The Redemption of God*, 7–9. Speaking to the importance of partnership, Heyward notes that, "to believe in God is to believe that God and humanity are together in this world, ultimately and immediately connected . . . A lover needs relation—if for no other reason, in order to love . . . In relation to God, as in any relation, God is affected by humanity and creation, just as we are affected by God."

With regard to the possible reasons for this reflection, see Coats, *Genesis*, 140, who suggests that, "The initial soliloquies relate to each other as opposites. The first sets out the divine plan to reveal to Abraham intentions for future plans: (1) Abraham holds the divine promise to become a great nation and thereby to provide a blessing to all the nations of the earth, and (2) Abraham holds a special position before God ("I have known him" [*yedaʿtîw*]). The purpose of the position is to maintain righteousness and justice in coming generations."

the general "outcry"). Again, without explicit emphasis by the narrator, the notion of the co-creatorship is undergirded.

Fourth, we note that no one particular crime or act of injustice in the lives of the Sodomites constitutes a justification for the compliant of an "outcry." Consequently, the narrator allows "outcry" to remain without a specific association with a crime. With this omission, the reader forfeits any and all opportunity to initiate investigatory procedures regarding not only the commission of such acts, but also the subsequent judgment imposed by Yahweh. We understand, further, that Yahweh will clearly not act on a second hand report. Yahweh will have to witness the situation personally before any action is taken. Whatever we may think of the grand scheme of life events in this world, this text grants us a glimpse of the intrinsic character of God; life is not fatalistic or predetermined. Judgment and destruction are not fated, even when based on the gravest of outcries. Abraham's discourse with God on Sodom's behalf would underline this understanding.

This is God portrayed in anthropomorphic fashion. Even so, one must be careful to articulate that this anthropomorphic God is a God actively involved in the lives of the people, and not a God who only wills destruction. As in Gen 11:5, where, in the context of the building of the tower of Babel, God comes down personally to determine the nature and the truth of the problem. Here too, God physically enters the realm of human beings and makes a decision determined by on-site observation. Indeed, God determines that a personal assessment of the situation is necessary. We know from the text that God is aware of the "outcry" and we also know that God has acted on an "outcry" when God has heard it (Exod. 3:7), but this situation is different. The nature and gravity of the "outcry" here prompts God to view the matter personally. It is not that God doubts, but the narrator underlines the significance of "seeing" versus "hearing" (e.g., Job 42:5; John 20:24–40).[33] Distinctively in this text, however, while God is fully aware of the "outcry," God is not particularly calculating in the matter of the punishment for Sodom and Gomorrah.

Fretheim submits that, "God has not *finally* determined that Sodom shall suffer doom . . . This divine if (*'im*) relates not to God's actual knowledge of the situation in Sodom, but to whether its inhabitants' behavior is commensurate with 'the outcry against' and what it no doubt

---

33. See the first speech of God in Job 38. Also Wiesel, *Twilight*, 207-8.

called for—namely destruction."³⁴ God clearly is not "trigger-happy" when it comes to judgment. This is a God who is actively involved in the lives of the people and is not intent on destruction. God physically enters the arena of humanity to have a sense of the manner in which life is lived. This text also portrays a striking image of the vulnerability of God, particularly in v. 21. God is not seen as overpowering and all powerful. That is not to say that God has no power, but it suggests that God takes seriously the difficulty of human life. While human beings remain unaware of the difficulty of what it means to be God, we see here the possibility that God also struggles with what it means to be human.

For the Sake of a Few

The narrator in this text is finally not interested in the theology of "how" with respect to the encounter between Yahweh and Abraham. Hence, though we are never told what transformation occurs that enables Abraham to recognize Yahweh, yet as the unit unfolds we know that Abraham is fully aware of the identity of the deity.

Brueggemann notes that in v. 22, the original text, prior to any translation, read, "Yahweh stood before Abraham," which inverts the common expectation.³⁵ The MT now reads "Abraham stood before Yahweh," which, in the estimation of the translators, is the correct posture for any kind of discourse between a human being and God.³⁶

It was determined earlier that this text confirms a partnership between Abraham and Yahweh; thus we are able to assert that the original text is in no way, beyond the scope of appropriate theological etiquette. Mindful that it is Yahweh who seeks to explore the "outcry" in Sodom, God standing before Abraham confirms a God interested in human

---

34. Fretheim, *The Suffering of God*, 49.

35. Brueggemann, *Genesis*, 168.

36. Brisman, *The Voice of Jacob*, 61: "The real force of Abraham's question in 18:24 may best be felt if one sees it as a reaction to the Eisaacic ["E" Source] trial of Abraham's faith. Eisaac pictures Elohim putting Abraham on trial. Jacob ["J"] reacts by picturing Abraham putting Yava on trial. It is curious that the most blatant support for this view has routinely been construed as a textual error: We read, "Yava stood before Abraham" (19:22) as though Yava stood on trial in the conversation that follows; but the text is conventionally emended, "Abraham stood before Yava" which it certainly would have read were Eisaac, not Jacob its author."

consideration and partnership.³⁷ The responsibility of being a blessing to all people occupies a central position in Abraham's heart and mind, and he accepts the responsibility with all seriousness. This becomes abundantly apparent when we hear Abraham take God to task (vv. 23–25). The challenge by Abraham is predicated on Abraham's belief that God is a God of grace and goodness, not only to Abraham and Sarah, but to all people. In God's contemplation of total annihilation of the two cities, Abraham expresses concern that fundamental elements of the partnership are being ignored or at least infracted. As Milgrom notes, "the emulation of God's holiness demands following the ethics associated with his nature."³⁸ The text allows us to argue with strong justification that Abraham takes seriously this, "walking in Yahweh's ethical footsteps."³⁹ We do not dare ignore the pointed juxtaposition contained herein. It is Yahweh who has established the charge and promise to Abraham, relative to a relationship of blessing to all people, and thus Yahweh calls Abraham to implicit trust and confidence. In response, Abraham offers extravagant hospitality to strangers who come to his door, ignoring all reference to character or identity, and serving them graciously and abundantly. Now in vv. 22ff, Abraham expects Yahweh, Abraham's partner, to walk in a similar, consistent manner.

Abraham's challenge to Yahweh underlines two essentials of this partnership which were not only initiated by God's graciousness, but further shaped by the very character of God: (1) that God is not a capricious God (2) that each participant in a partnership holds the right, and responsibility of calling the other to account in the case of alleged or actual acts of injustice. The issue at stake here is whether God will indeed destroy the righteous along with the wicked. One should not assume that Abraham is calling God to cease all punishment of people regardless of their actions. Gutierrez correctly maintains that, "grace is not opposed to the quest for justice nor does it play it down; on the contrary, it gives it full meaning. God's love like all true love operates

37. Fretheim, *The Suffering of God*, 49.
38. Milgrom, "The Biblical Diet Laws," 293.
39. Having noted the insistence by Abraham that the actions of Yahweh reflect the expectations placed upon Abraham, it is Abraham who broaches the subject of punishment (vv. 23ff.). According to this text, Abraham is the one who comes to the conclusion that Yahweh will completely annihilate Sodom. This conclusion is not much different in its audacity, than the disbelief of Sarah when she hears of the promise of a son. Both expressions of audacity reflect the notion that certain realities are fixed.

in a world not of cause and effect, but of freedom and gratuitousness."[40] What the narrator cleverly inserts in this text is the notion that both Yahweh and Abraham are functioning on the same wavelength. In v. 21 it is the righteous character of God that would not allow God to destroy these cities without first entering them. In approaching Abraham's challenge to Yahweh, there are two theological issues to be considered.

First, there is the matter of God's identity. The name of God simply cannot be profaned. Total destruction of Sodom and Gomorrah would place the integrity of God's name in deep jeopardy (see Ezek 20:9). In sharp relief, the scenario created by the narrator pits the righteousness of God against the profanity of the destruction of righteous people, thus strongly emphasizing the irreconcilable difference created. In this regard, v. 25 has Abraham calling this matter to God's attention twice. In the eyes of Abraham God is incapable of injustice and unrighteousness. Abraham imagines that some righteous people live in Sodom and Gomorrah and the destruction of the righteous with the wicked constitutes injustice, thus defaming the name and identity of Yahweh.

There is a second, equally important theological issue. The attitude and response of contiguous nations must be acknowledged, if indeed Abraham will be allowed to carry out the explicit and implicit elements of the promise to be a blessing. Terrien is surely right when he observes that, "the Yahwist theologian deliberately inserted the promise of Abraham's posterity within the universal vision of Heilsgeschichte."[41] One might say that Abraham reminds God that God would have to consider what the neighbors will think. This is not simply some kind of flimsy excuse, but an essential component of the intent of God (see Exod 31:12).

A Matter of Stopping Short

The discourse between Abraham and God in vv. 22–33 is one of the more extraordinary biblical encounters involving the divine and human. Of primary importance is the dialogical nature of the text. Gammie submits that it is untenable to think of biblical proclamation apart from a dia-

---

40. Gutierrez, *On Job*, 87. See also Boff, *Church*, 51, who notes that the power of love is, "different in nature from the power of domination; it is fragile, vulnerable, conquering through its weakness and its capacity for giving and forgiveness. Jesus always demonstrated this *exousia* in his life."

41. Terrien, *The Elusive Presence*, 81.

logical dimension.⁴² There are several items to note in this regard. First, Abraham, trusting his right and ability to dialogue with God, broaches the subject of the righteous being destroyed along with the wicked and the number fifty is in the first instance used by Abraham in a hypothetical way (v. 24). Yahweh immediately makes the move from probability to concreteness, taking the same number as a point of departure, as Yahweh answers Abraham. This same number is then taken by Yahweh as the point of departure for answering the question of Abraham (v. 26). Right from the start, the issue in the mind of Abraham is the righteousness of God and not so much the righteousness of the people of Sodom.⁴³ The reality is that whatever happens by way of grace, it would be the initiative of God and not of the people. One recalls the situation with Nineveh, where despite the reluctance of Jonah, the Ninevites are nevertheless given a chance for repentance. In the case of Sodom, there is no such deliberation. If Sodom is going to be saved, it would be an act of grace by God. In v. 26, God responds to Abraham's request by saying that the entire city will be forgiven (spared, RSV). The theologian at work in this text seeks to articulate Yahweh as the voice of grace, setting no logical basis for the decision regarding destruction.

Second, the word in v. 23, which the RSV translates "destroy" and the NRSV "sweep away" is rich in meaning and aids the reader in coming to grips with the severity of the situation. This same word is found in Gen 19:15,17 and is translated by the RSV as "consume." "Consume" paints a picture of finality and obliteration.⁴⁴ The point of interest here is

42. Gammie, *Holiness in Israel*, 94.

43. See, Lawrence A. Turner, *Announcements of Plot in Genesis*. JSOT Press, 1990. Turner argues that, "Before the birth of Isaac-should he ever be born-Abraham has two 'half chances' in Ishmael and Lot, and he wishes to preserve them at all costs. This explains why he circumcises Ishmael and pleads for Sodom. I would suggest that Abraham's plea to save the whole city on ethical grounds is motivated largely by a desire to save his nephew and his potential heir." pp. 79-80. It seems to me that Turner misses the point of the narrative. For Abraham to proceed on these grounds is to create a perverse ulterior motive, and it brings into serious question the role of Abraham as the ancestor of faith. Whatever else one might attribute to Abraham by way of his flaws, it is not apparent that he is "hedging his bets" by feigning care and compassion.

44. The corresponding Arabic term has the meaning of being driven away by a strong wind or something of a dust storm. In light of the Gen 19:23ff. description that speaks of raining sulphur and fire from heaven and further (v. 28), when Abraham observes "the smoke of the land going up like the smoke of a furnace," even the Arabic term does not begin to capture the essence of the destruction. Perhaps it is safe to say that one cannot begin to image the finality of the destruction unless it is personally witnessed.

that Sodom faces the possibility of being wiped out in a manner where there is no trace of prior existence. There is a tone of finality.

A third issue is the description of Yahweh as judge of all the earth, one who relates to communities as well as individuals. Von Rad concludes that the concern of the theologian here, is for the community, moving beyond the scope of individual righteousness.[45] While the narrator gives clear definition to the issue of individual righteousness versus individual evil, the focus changes when the object becomes the object of judgment, as in the case of Sodom. This is more than a tangential issue.

How will God deal with a community which departs from all relationship expectations? In the punishment handed down, will the innocent be destroyed along with the guilty? Counted among the innocent would be members of the community who may have themselves been the victims of earlier human injustices. Will they now become objects of divine injustice as well? If this were to be the case, then God might surely be characterized as capricious and void of justice.[46] The God with whom Abraham is in partnership is not such a God and Abraham would seek to remind God of this.[47]

Sodom, Lot's home by choice (Gen 13:8–13) might be regarded as a community of outsiders. That is to say, they were not partners in the covenant relation with Yahweh. However, responsibilities of relationship are expected of all people, as they live in community. The Sodom of Genesis bears resemblance to the Israel of Amos 2, with one notable distinction. In Genesis 19, the city inhabitants treat sojourners and visitors with a violence equal to that which they demonstrate to each other. The lack of hospitality on the part of the Sodomites stands in sharp contrast to the earlier hospitable act of Abraham and Sarah to the visitors.

Finally, we note that Abraham dares to "push his luck" with God. This is one of the more difficult elements for contemporary believers to grasp. Many abhor the notion of challenging God, to the point of believing that it is sacrilegious to do so. More than anything, the chal-

---

45. Von Rad, *Old Testament Theology*, 394–95.

46. See Jung, *Answer to Job*, 7ff., who argues that God is not capricious, but he sees God as one who indeed metes out and allows unjust suffering.

47. See Alter, "Sodom as Nexus," 150, who notes that it is the doing of 'righteousness and justice' (Gen 18:19) that are expected of Abraham, which Abraham comes to expect of God.

lenge here posits the relationship in positive light, indeed a position with inherent integrity. In any valid relationship, one has to have the confidence to pursue that which is true, even if it involves challenging systemic and imperial power and those who represent the status quo. Inevitably one risks the consequential ending of the relationship. Indeed if Abraham were to bypass the questioning of God here, he would be delinquent in his relationship.

The text invites the reader to witness the courage of Abraham in this challenge to God, as multiple references are made to the fear experienced by Abraham during the encounter. He is surely fearful of the potential response of Yahweh. Twice Abraham recalls his humanity in the face of Yahweh's divinity (vv. 27, 31). While this is not a suggestion that Abraham is reconsidering, Abraham thus recognizes the distinction between the divinity of Yahweh and his own finitude. The language of "dust and ashes" in v. 27 underlines this. Abraham recognizes his own humanity. Before any conversation takes place, Abraham acknowledges that he is indeed a part of God's created order, of dust and ashes. Further, twice Abraham pleads with God not to be angry with him (vv. 30, 32). The element of fear is not peripheral or imagined. Abraham is embarking on unknown territory here and in the realm of journeying, he discovers the lengths to which he might go along with the danger of the unknown. Yet, Abraham remains undaunted, for in the pursuit of righteous deeds, he recognizes the probability of encounters with the unknown, with fear, and with the powerful.

The narrator is precise in alerting the reader to the fact that Abraham, not Yahweh is the initiator of the discussion on righteous behavior and the call to protect the name of Yahweh stands always as the respondent to the challenge. One might contend that Abraham is "ecstatic" in his manner of relating to God. Taking this term literally, he stands outside of himself in this discourse; he is not concerned about *his* righteousness, but nevertheless has the audacity to confront Yahweh's righteousness. This ecstatic nature of Abraham pushes him to take risks in order to pursue that which he has been led to believe was right and just. In this encounter with God, we see that risk and trust are not unevenly yoked; indeed they walk hand-in-hand, side-by-side. In order for there to be newness, there would need to be risk and inherent in this risk is trust. Abraham, with all his questions, took an essential risk. In all of this, Abraham might appear to the reader to be somewhat arrogant in this encounter, but indeed he is taking seriously the task to which he has been called.

As the narrator establishes in v. 21, Yahweh is about to go to Sodom and ascertain the level of the outcry before making any kind of pronouncement.[48] As the discourse between Yahweh and Abraham develops, there is no discussion or argumentation on the part of Yahweh. It is Abraham who asks and, without ever departing from what has become a standard answer, Yahweh agrees to Abraham's terms. What must be remembered here is the narrator's clear intimation that Yahweh as yet has not seen the situation in Sodom. That Yahweh is immediately ready to forgive the sin of Sodom for the sake of the righteous present, attests the righteousness of Yahweh. It is not to be assumed that Yahweh already knows that Sodom is void of any righteous person. Rather, one would emphasize the gracious and righteous nature of Yahweh.[49]

Moreover, even as the fear in the heart of Abraham mounts, he yet pleads with God on behalf of Sodom. Present here is the rare combination of fear and ecstasy on the part of Abraham.[50] There are two singularly important points to note in this regard.

First, nothing in the text, whether Yahweh's words or tone of voice suggests to Abraham that Yahweh is becoming tired of the ensuing negotiation. The theologian at work carefully demonstrates a consis-

---

48. Brisman, *The Voice of Jacob*, 61: "In the Sodom story, Abraham asks, *haʿap tispeh weloʾ-tiśśaʾ lamaqom*. Will you destroy and not carry away [the iniquity of] the place? (18:24) This sentence has its own verbal play, for both *tispeh* and *tiśśaʾ* can mean "carry away." In context, *tispeh* means "snatch away from the face of the earth"—destroying the whole city because of the wicked inhabitants in it. Abraham questions whether the righteous will be snatched away with the wicked, whether God will not rather "bear away" the iniquity of the city as a whole, thus freeing the place from the burden of guilt of some of its inhabitants. The question constitutes not just a humble plea for mercy but a little trial of Yava's justice: Which kind of "carrying away" is truest to your nature Yava? Are you a god who tests people's faith, or is your nature to grant the benefit of the doubt?"

49. Contra Coats, "Lot: A Foil in the Abraham Narrative," 120, who argues that the essence of the bargaining is that "not even ten righteous people could be found in Sodom." Also Brisman, *The Voice of Jacob*, 44: "we can best understand the Jacobic tale of Abraham bargaining with Yava as a midrash or a set of midrashim on an 'already written' fate of Sodom." To sustain a view such as Brisman's is to suggest that Yahweh was engaging Abraham in a discourse about life and death issues, where 'death' has already been determined. In light of the partnership motif in the text and the inherent integrity therein, Brisman's position would appear untenable.

50. One might note other biblical scenarios where fear and ecstasy are in deep tension, e.g., the meeting between Ruth and Boaz in the house of Boaz (Ruth 3:6ff.).

tency of response by Yahweh, which exhibits neither dissatisfaction nor weariness. Consequently, perhaps the fear expressed by Abraham serves to mark the persistent distance between God and humanity. Such a distance carries necessary and positive connotations.

The second issue to note is the abrupt ending of the dialogue. Though Abraham has given warning that he is about to end his query of Yahweh, the reader is unprepared for the cessation of Abraham's pleas. This abrupt characteristic carries even greater significance, when we recall the conspicuous lack of impatience on the part of Yahweh, who gave no intimation of an unwillingness to continue the dialogue. Hence, Abraham might have carried the discourse to a logical conclusion, namely: would God spare Sodom for the sake of one righteous person.

Instead, Abraham ceases to pursue after Yahweh agrees to save Sodom for the sake of ten righteous. This is extraordinary on two counts. In the first place, Abraham for the sake of righteousness, challenged God to refrain from totally obliterating this city. To this challenge, Yahweh without exception responds with grace. Further, it is Abraham who brings the discourse to an end. This has great implications for all humanity. What Abraham has done by ending the conversation with God is to imply that perhaps God, when pushed to the limit might respond adversely. The implicit fear and distrust here must not go unnoticed. In reality, Yahweh without ever indicating an alternate response, accepted the challenge to save the city for the sake of ten. One might very well ask, how would Yahweh respond had Abraham asked: "And if one righteous person is found? What then Lord, will you destroy Sodom?" for the sake of one. Indeed, we are surprised that Abraham does not pursue this any further, given the fact that he was aware that Lot was in Sodom. Though one may only speculate here, the reader has ample basis to believe that God would have saved the city.

To this extent therefore, we must connect this abruptness and lack of trust on the part of Abraham to the response of Yahweh, to the laughter and disbelief of Sarah. "Is anything too wonderful for the LORD?" (v. 14a). The RSV focuses on the *difficulty* of the situation. Even though scholars such as Westermann opt for the reading of *difficult*,[51] the issue at stake in both of these instances is hardly the level of difficulty. Indeed difficulty is never really the issue. The underlying crux is the belief in a God who does indeed work wonders. By ending the discourse,

---

51. Westermann. *Genesis 12–36*, 281.

Abraham is led to believe, as are we, that Yahweh would not respond with any wonder. Human lack of imagination has thus not only characterized Abraham's pursuit, but shaped the manner in which Abraham understands God's role. The danger here in great part has to do with the limited vision with which human beings view the capacity of God to do that which is borne out of grace and does not hinge on human action. The promise for those of us who would seek to immerse ourselves in this story is that God is willing to go beyond our wildest imagination. Part of what Abraham suffers from is a lack of imagination. While he is willing to challenge God for that which is noble, he stops short of imagining a future that is shaped singularly by the grace and hospitality of God. One is indeed led to believe that in counter distinction to the explicit challenge of God by Abraham, is the implicit challenge by God of Abraham, and to all humanity, to push God to the limit and believe that God will respond graciously. While God is willing to pursue the goal further, Abraham stops short. The particularity of Abraham's situation serves as a metaphor for humanity in general. The focus is not so much on the finite nature of the human, but on the limitation which human finitude places on the extent to which God will act even for those who are utterly undeserving.

As we come to the end of this text we cannot but shift the focus of our thoughts to the New Testament, where in the person of Jesus the Messiah we indeed have one who is totally righteous. What God does in Christ is to remind the world of the extent to which God would go to bring life to those who are undeserving. Moreover, if we were to take the case of Abraham who sought to have God reflect on the possibility of saving an undeserving people on the basis of a few righteous and yet stopped short, we would come face to face with the reality that God has acted beyond human imagination. What God did with one righteous person was inconceivable even to one human who challenged God to reconsider.

To be sure the hospitality of Abraham and Sarah is exemplary, but when all is said and done, the grace that comes again and again and startles humanity is the grace which shatters human imagination.

3

On Choosing Death

Genesis 19

SCHOLARLY CONSENSUS UNDERSTANDS THE TEXT OF GENESIS 19 AS a chronological forerunner to Genesis 18. Indeed the portrayal of Yahweh in Genesis 18 may very well serve as a response to the material in Genesis 19. However, the discussion that follows is not shaped by this kind of chronology. Instead we shall explore the direction of the narrator seeking to comprehend the theological trajectories that are developed in Genesis 19. As with Genesis 18 society has seen fit to overwork particular themes of Genesis 19 to the natural detriment, even exclusion of other themes. Homosexuality serves as an example here of such a misconstrued central theme. In actuality, while one would not want to overlook the issue as a function within the text, this theme has no centrality in the narrator's thought-progression in the story. This chapter focuses rather, I would suggest, on the powerful, though often ignored theme of hospitality in light of the larger framework of the tension between central and marginal existence. Indeed while hospitality is often made to be a marginalized issue by society and tradition, any other so-called centralized issue in this text must be understood from the notion of hospitality. Understanding the implications of hospitality in this particular context (hospitality offered, hospitality refused, hospitality withheld, hospitality distorted and perverted) carries the potentiality of impacting and shaping one's theology with new and biblically authentic integrity.[1]

---

1. Brueggemann, *Power, Providence and Personality*, 49, notes that, "The theme of power rooted in violence is pervasively evident in the contemporary world. As sexism and racism are exposed, and disadvantaged peoples no longer accept conventional in-

Given the fact that this text is not to be understood in isolation, a brief comparison between the hospitality of Abraham and Lot will help set the scene.[2]

Abraham and Lot

According to Gen 18:1–2, Abraham ran to greet the visitors "in the heat of the day." This gesture, along with the specified time of day would set the scene, defining the constitutive elements of Abraham's hospitality. In rather sharp contrast to this, the narrator of Gen 19:1, employing the temporal phrase "in the evening," carefully and precisely indicates a more comfortable, leisurely time of day. While Lot cannot be faulted for this temporal setting, we have an immediate though subtle indication that this act of hospitality will be different from that of Abraham.[3]

While "he rose to meet them" (19:1) hardly denotes a sinister approach, the absence here of the urgent language so characteristic of Abraham actions, strikes the reader. One of the directions of this chapter is to demonstrate that despite the focus that is placed on Lot, and the responsibility for life that he carries, his actions are less than laudable. From the very beginning of the story, even as the scene is set for us, the narrator intentionally alerts us to the startling lack of urgency in Lot's actions.

---

equities, the connection between power and violence is starkly evident." Brueggemann's observation is surely applicable to the biblical text under study here. The scene is that of an entire city about to abuse a couple of visitors, powerless not only in numbers, but clearly because they were outsiders—in a strange place and among, as it turned out, hostile residents. Moreover, they become hostile and abusive against the host who has lived in the midst for a while, but nevertheless was reminded that he was a sojourner. This conclusion of Brueggemann is also applicable to Lot who demonstrated the power which he had over his family and is willing to bring about violence against his own daughters in a manner that any parent would find reprehensible.

2. Rosenberg, *King and Kin*, 77, notes that, "Lot's hospitality, while certainly as generous in main outline as Abraham's (and in one respect, 19:8, more so), is a poor copy of his kinsman. His willingness to sacrifice his daughters (and thus his posterity) to the whim of the Sodomites stands in bold contrast to the importance of a posterity to Abraham." Following on this, one might conclude that Lot is willing to sacrifice his future for the sake of his present, personal safety.

3. Alexander, "Lot's Hospitality," 290, perceives greater, though superficial similarities between Abraham and Lot. He notes, "Initially both men are seated: Abraham at the door of the tent (18:1); Lot at the gate of the city (19:1). On observing the approach of some strangers, they arise, greet them, and bowing to the ground graciously extend an offer of hospitality. Even their speeches correspond closely."

Scattered nuances in the narrative might suggest that Lot was in a state of hurriedness, yet further exploration reveals that perhaps the "haste" might have been for the sake of Lot's personal safety and not for those who were around him.[4] One might push this even further noting that the narrator intentionally creates a collage of Lot suggestive of anything but urgency.[5] Even so, we do not wish to conclude that Lot was unaware of the appropriate manner of greeting the visitors, as dictated by his culture. Though he bows to the ground in greeting, his subsequent actions demonstrate that he is intent on proceeding with his personal agenda, ignoring the interests of the guests.

Compare the invitation of Abraham and Lot. In 18:3 Abraham greets the strangers with the statement, "My lord if I find favor with you, do not pass by your servant." In 19:2 Lot's invitation is described thus: "Please, my lords turn aside to your servant's house and spend the night, and wash your feet; then you can rise early and go on your way." On a superficial level, one might note that Abraham's invitation is general, while Lot's is much more specific. Generality and specificity only in and of themselves are not to be equated with acceptable levels of hospitality. In the invitation of Abraham, there is a notable respect of the dignity of the strangers and in so doing, Abraham ensures that the identity of the strangers is not diminished for the sake of hospitality provided. The strangers are consulted before Abraham proceeds to do what was necessary. The essential "if" (*'im*) in Abraham's greeting sets it in contradistinction to the invitation of Lot.

On the other hand, one senses that Lot has an established agenda. Granted, he invites the strangers into his house, yet they are given no opportunity to make a decision on their own behalf. As we have noted previously, the nature of extending hospitality to others excludes all intimations of condescension. Hospitality loses its intrinsic nature, which includes invitation, when conditions are forced upon the recipient. Coercion is never to be a part of hospitality. As intrinsic as invitation is to hospitality, so is coercion intrinsic to hostility. The distinction

---

4. However, one notes that later when Lot is urged by the guests to get out of Sodom, he lingers and places at risk not only the lives of his family, but his own. It would appear that at least textually, Lot is inconsistent.

5. Throughout this study, I shall be distinguishing between "urgency" and "hurriedness." While the former is attributed to Abraham in his approach to the visitors, "hurriedness" is the term which best describes Lot. Haste/hurriedness is more suggestive of sloppiness, and perhaps here the pursuing of one's own agenda.

between these two may be subtle, for often hospitality, the act itself deceptively obscures the coerciveness of the invitation and prescribed direction of the host.

Moreover, the extravagance of Abraham stands in sharp contrast to Lot's meager, hasty offering. Initially, the offer of rest dominates the invitation of Lot, together with the washing of the feet. Both of these are important components of hospitality, though, the specific absence of a meal delineates the difference between Abraham and Lot. Only *after* Lot insists that the strangers stay with him are we told that he prepares a feast for them.

We will consider two specific Hebrew words that may serve to highlight the sharp contrast between Lot and Abraham. Even here the general Hebrew term *mishteh* is used for "feast" and the narrator in no way emphasizes the specific items of the menu. *Maššôt* is the only food that is specified, whereas, in the wondrous, extravagant meal prepared by Abraham and Sarah, we were told by numerous tantalizing adjectives of the gourmet quality and quantity of the ingredients of the food, and further, the meticulous care taken in the preparation thereof. The use of *mišteh* clues us to Lot's less than meticulous preparation. One cannot help but contrast the detailed, urgent preparation of Abraham and the tentative general plans of Lot.

Abraham offers "a morsel of bread"—*pat-leḥem*, while Lot made a "feast" (*mišteh*) consisting of "unleavened bread" (*maṣṣôt*). Is this already a notion of Abraham's "understanding" of extravagant hospitality, while Lot would tend to overstate his own generosity? Often those who are generous (even extravagant by the standards of society), offering far more than is needed or expected, would never characterize themselves as "generous"—they simply offer what seems appropriate to the circumstance. In stark contrast, those who tend to be selfish perceive even the little that they offer as an indication of their magnanimous nature.

Further careful consideration of these two Hebrew words, *mishteh* and *maṣṣôt* may prove helpful as we attempt to discern more precisely, the textual implications of this contrast in modes of hospitality, as exhibited by Abraham and Lot. The general biblical understanding of *mishteh* is a feast with wine, though Westermann translates this term, "meal."[6] We note with interest that in pointing to the fact that Lot prepared a feast, immediately following this, the narrator specifies the baking of

---

6. Westermann, *Genesis 12–36*, 295.

maṣṣôt. Whatever else the narrator might have in mind, the mentioning of *maṣṣôt* hardly points to extravagance or "feast" on the part of Lot.[7] "Feast" implies, even necessitates lengthy, detailed preparation, while one advantage of *maṣṣôt* is that the time needed for preparation is minimal. Though the *mišteh* ("feast") is totally absent in the Genesis 18 narrative, the detailed description, not only of Abraham's own part in the preparation, but also his explicit directives to Sarah and the servants, suggest "feast" as far more than the abbreviated treatment given to the food, consisting singularly of *maṣṣôt*, which is to be consumed in Genesis 19.

In unfurling one's imagination, one finds two positive overtones that derive from the use of *maṣṣôt* in this text. First, we are allowed a preview of the danger that Lot and the strangers face, as well as a foretaste of the deliverance which they will receive from God. To be sure, the presence of *maṣṣôt* here is but a single feature, reflecting the grand act of deliverance as recorded in the exodus event, but this presence powerfully pinpoints the gravity of the situation soon to be experienced by Lot and the strangers. As we shall see, Lot remains unaware of this very gravity throughout the narrative. In any event, the presence of the *maṣṣôt* and its association with the deliverance from Egypt emphasizes the importance of remembering, a theme which undergirds the Israelite narratives.

Second, *maṣṣôt* is baked "in haste." As in the account of the exodus event, haste is an imperative, not an option. This reference to haste provides a harbinger of the manner in which Lot and his family will have to leave the city if they want to be spared being victims of the devastating destruction.

In unusual and noteworthy exclusivity, Lot in no way engages the family in the act of hospitality, but rather seeks to do everything himself. The exclusivity here places Lot in a less than flattering light. When other members of the family enter the scene later, they are being used in ways that place them in grave danger. As we contrast the act of Abraham we recall that Sarah along with other members of the household participate in the activities of caring for the strangers. The singularity of Lot providing the feast is not a reflection of the narrator's intent in showing the egalitarian nature of Lot. Israelite tradition necessitated that women and servants prepare the food. Such a strict limitation may, indeed, be too restrictive and thus, unacceptable for contemporary western marriage

---

7. Jeansonne, *The Women of Genesis*, 34, observes that the baking of unleavened bread recalls the bread made under dire circumstances in Egypt as the Israelites fled from their enemies in haste.

patterns and sensibilities. Be that as it may, within the text, we note the additional irony in the failure to make even a passing reference to the work done by Lot's wife and daughters. This pointed omission alerts us to the fact that, as intentionally portrayed by the narrator, Lot is a flawed character, not only in his relationship to outsiders and relatives, but also as he deals with the intimate members of his immediate family.

One further note: Lot clearly sets his boundaries. As indicated earlier, the essential "if" that we find in the greeting of Abraham (Gen 18:3) is missing in Lot's greeting. In 19:2, following the initial invitation, Lot gives permission to the strangers to wash themselves and rest, since they need to rise early in the morning and be on their way. We do not hear the visitors articulate their plans, as Lot never bothers to ask, and further, he does not allow them the opportunity to remain with him any longer than the bare minimum time. The use of temporal references both in vv. 1 and 2 bring the brevity of the strangers' welcome into sharp relief. One cannot help but get the impression that Lot continues to work with a set, and prescribed agenda. Nothing in the manner in which he treats the strangers suggests that he is interested in going beyond the bare essentials. The notion of something ordinary is at work here. In other words, there is no going beyond that which is required. While it is true that a meal to a hungry individual is in itself life giving, the attitude of Lot indicates that he sets strict limits, beyond which he refuses to go.

Essential to the development of this story is the immediate realization that Lot is no Abraham and indeed significant and sufficient differences cast doubts over the integrity and decency of Lot. As the story unfolds we come to the knowledge that Lot leaves a great deal to be desired with regard to hospitality both to outsiders and to members of his family.

A City Engulfed in Violence

Lot's response to the strangers' suggestion that they will spend the night in the square moves beyond what is customary for oriental hospitality. His insistence overrides the degree to which an invitation might be pushed. Jeansonne suggests that, "wittingly or unwittingly, Lot's suggestion that they stay with him instead of in the street has the potential to thwart the divine plan."[8]

8. Ibid., 35. While Jeansonne poses an insightful proposition, there is another

The narrator's use of "pressed hard" (*pṣr*) in describing Lot's insistence is particularly significant as this is the term which is also used to describe the pressure exerted on Lot by the men of Sodom.⁹ This latter use of *pṣr* in v. 9b inevitably comes to bear on the direction of its use in v. 3a.¹⁰ The reality is that because of Lot's relentless "pushing" the visitors are not given the opportunity to make a decision on their own. Coercion is subtly substituted for invitation. Later, the men of Sodom are not subtle in their insistence and this time, Lot in similar fashion is disallowed from making a decision on his own accord.¹¹

The sense of impending doom graphically and sharply described by the narrator through the four-fold progression in v. 4, not only heightens the drama of the extent of the imminent violence, but draws attention to the fact that violence enveloped the entire city of Sodom. The narrator goes to great lengths to ensure that no doubt exists in the minds of the readers. The overwhelming shadow of wickedness prompts the use of "outcry" as a way of dramatically describing the state of affairs in Sodom. The language of being "surrounded" further intensifies the desperate and hopeless situation. In today's vernacular, the notion of "surrounded" rings of being overcome: a particular defense coming to an end. Being "surrounded" carries the inevitable overtones of surrender, loss and defeat. The fact that the men surrounded the house of Lot surely spells an ominous end.¹²

---

direction that one might take this. Through staying with Lot, the visitors received a first hand experience of the "outcry," without actually becoming victims of the violence. We recall that the intent of this visit was to determine the level of the "outcry" personally. (18:21) One could only deduce here that the knowledge of the visitors' presence was widespread and remaining in the street would surely have resulted in their deaths. At least in the light of the narrative, it seems entirely plausible that had the visitors remained in the streets they would have been gang raped and murdered.

9. Note Luther, *Lectures on Genesis 15–20*, 246. Luther in attempting to defend the insistence of Lot says, "[Lot] insists when they decline, for he feared for them because of the citizens." If this were true of Lot, then his actions later in sacrificing his daughters is doubly troublesome, for then surely it suggests that he knew precisely the level of danger he was about to cast his daughters into.

10. The irony here is that it is only in v. 3a that Lot is described as acting urgently (see RSV and NRSV). His strong urging of the visitors to stay with him will come to serve as a sharp contrast to his later actions, where in the face of death, he lingers.

11. See also a similar use of *pṣr* in Judg 19:22.

12. See Brisman, *The Voice of Jacob*, 62, who notes a parallel between the visit of Yahweh to "see" the outcry in Sodom, thereby knowing with certainty the situation, and a perverse parallel of this by the Sodomites who wish to "know" the visitors.

The intention of the men of Sodom is not shrouded in any kind of ambiguity. Even though some scholars have suggested that "know" (*yd'*) in this context implies an interest in being acquainted with the strangers, no such intimation can be drawn from the text.[13] The hostility and evil intent in surrounding Lot's house indicate that this was far from being a well-meaning visit; this is not a welcoming party. The visit was shrouded in hostility, and the only intent was to rape the male visitors![14]

The all male constituency of the group of Sodomites, reflects the dominance and the underlying subservience of the women in the society. One might draw any number of conclusions regarding the absence of women; and one that has been propounded regularly is the men's interest in a homosexual encounter. Consequently, the presence of the women in this context would not fit the atmosphere of the narrative. Such a narrow view surely overlooks the textual violence against the women. Their identities were subsumed through the dominance of the men. One might also surmise in this regard that perhaps this attitude towards the visitors would not be tolerated by the women of Sodom, if for no other reason that they themselves would recognize the violence which was about to take place.

We can begin to understand this incident by assuming that not all the men of Sodom were homosexual in sexual orientation. Indeed we know from the text that the sons-in-law lived in the city and they were engaged to be married to the daughters of Lot. That some of the men were homosexual is probable; that all the men of the city were homosexual is virtually impossible.[15] The intent of the author is not in any way to demonstrate that the "outcry" of the city was the presence of homosexuality. That is simply not the point of the story. The focus of this narrative is on domination and humiliation; of crushing others

---

13. See Bailey, *Homosexuality and the Western Christian Tradition*, 1–28.

14. See Tapp, "An Ideology of Expendability," 162: "The issue is not merely one of sex, it is more one of violence. As in any rape, and especially gang rape, sex is the vehicle through which violence and hatred are expressed. To emphasize 'sex' more than 'violence' denies the reality of the situation. The victims of the mob are threatened with physical violence (perhaps to the point of death) as well as sexual degradation."

15. See Clark and Richardson, "The *Malleus Maleficarum*," 119. The authors quote Trevor Roper whose comments were made in connection with the medieval persecution of women as witches, but are germane to the present discussion. "When a 'great fear' takes hold of society, that society looks naturally to the stereotype of the enemy in its midst."

who might be perceived to be different and weak. This is an act of utter violence seeking to be camouflaged through homosexuality.[16]

Not unlike the kind of power wielded by the Pharaoh and the Egyptians while the Hebrews were held in bondage, so too the men of Sodom wield an "imperial" power in the face of Lot's hospitality. Similarly, this text leads one to conclude that in the light of the overpowering presence of the Sodomites, at home in their native land, there is little potential for life for outsiders. The strangers as marginalized are viewed as objects. Names are not known; faces are not seen! Anonymity further attests the reduction of the strangers as objects. It is at this juncture, where death is "on the doorsteps" that a third party enters the picture. The angels who, to this point were the objects of the Sodomites' violence, now become the transformative force in the narrative. In the blinding of the Sodomites the power to perceive, and subsequently act, is negated. Alter observes that "the taboo against seeing has regular sexual associations in the Bible (as, of course, it also does in psychoanalytic terms). To 'see the nakedness' of someone is the standard biblical euphemism for incest. Genesis 19 does not use that idiom, but this rampant mob struck with blindness at a closed door is, after all, seeking forbidden sexual congress, and the story ends with a tale of incest."[17] Not only is Lot silenced; so too are the Sodomites. Brueggemann employs the metaphor of "intimidation," when speaking about the power of Yahweh over humans who use their power over others in destructive ways. The negative overtones of uncompromising brutality accompanying this use of intimidation describe the men of Sodom.[18] According to Brueggemann, the absolute quality of this sort of intrusion by Yahweh shifts the balance of power from one party to another and thereby delegitimizes the oppressor.[19]

Lot's offering of his virgin daughters reflects the societal values[20] where men were held in higher esteem than women and more valued

---

16. See Scanzoni and Mollenkott, *Is the Homosexual my Neighbor?* 57. According to these authors, "the Sodom story seems to be focusing on two specific evils: (1) violent gang rape and (2) inhospitality to the stranger."

17. Alter, "Sodom as Nexus," 152.

18. See Brueggemann. "The Transformative Potential of a Public Metaphor."

19. See Brueggemann, "The Embarrassing Footnote," 11ff.

20. See Lerner, *The Creation of Patriarchy*, 173, who suggests that, "If we analyze this Biblical story, we note that Lot's right to dispose of his daughters, even so as to offer them to be raped, is taken for granted. It does not need to be explained, hence we can assume that it reflected a historic social condition." *The Creation of Patriarchy*.

than women. From this episode, not only are men held in greater esteem, but a distorted notion of hospitality is given higher billing than the atrocity of violence. Further, not only are men held in higher esteem, but women are created for the purpose of being, in terms explicitly sexual and otherwise, "in service" to men. This notion is inherently related to this text, not only because of the protection of the male visitors, reflecting the "supremacy" of men, but perhaps more importantly, Lot's invitation to the men of Sodom to take his daughters.[21] One is led to conclude that the women should/could/must serve the needs of the men.[22] Moreover, great import has to be placed on the fact that the daughters had hitherto "not known a man;" this surely heightens the otherwise absent element of extravagant hospitality.[23] Lot's actions are primarily motivated by a concern for personal credibility in the eyes of others. After all, the idea of caring for the stranger was an integral component of Ancient Near Eastern life.

A number of ancient texts speak of the goodness and the righteousness of Lot. In Wisdom of Solomon 10, Lot is catalogued alongside Abraham, Noah, Joseph and Jacob as one of the righteous ancestors. References such as this are in large part responsible for the favorable opinion of some scholars regarding the character of Lot.[24] The principal argument that Lot proposes is that the men, "have come under the shelter of my roof" (v. 8b).

Lot has determined that hospitality is of paramount importance.[25] His act of protection of those who are strangers stands in sharp and

21. Clark and Richardson, "The *Malleus Maleficarum*," 28, observe: "Fathers, apparently, had the right to dispose of their children as they see fit."

22. This notion has been picked up over the years and made a part of acceptable norm. See Wiesner, "Luther and Women," 123, who quotes Luther: "Women are created for no other purpose than to serve men and be their helpers. If women grow weary or even die while bearing children, that doesn't harm anything. Let them bear children to death; they are created for that."

23. See Deut 22:23–27, which not only outlines the legal implications, but throughout, makes clear that the whole episode in Sodom wreaks of death. Also, Tapp, "An Ideology of Expendability," 168, notes that, "the sexual 'ripeness' of virgins simply enhances the hosts' compromise."

24. See, e.g., Alexander, "Lot's Hospitality," 290–91, who concludes that, "Lot is . . . to be viewed in a favorable light. Lot's hospitality is a mark of his righteousness . . . Concerning the events in Sodom, we should not judge too harshly a man placed in an extremely dangerous and apparently impossible situation."

25. Coats, "Lot," 121, underlines this notion: "Lot responds to the threat as a host should." On the heels of this statement, Coats does note that Lot's actions are hardly

disturbing contrast to those who are members of his own family. This is a distorted and perverted hospitality, and this sort of protection is actually no protection, for with such flawed priorities, one can surely imagine that even the protection of the stranger would be disposable in the face of some other priority. The daughters, his own flesh and blood, he readily sacrifices in a most violent way. The essence of caring, showing hospitality to strangers or outsiders or neighbors, is to do precisely that which one would do for oneself and one's own. Care for strangers is predicated on care for oneself. Lot's actions invert this to the point where hospitality becomes ludicrous. Violence of any kind must never be an element of hospitality; even further removed is a pseudo-hospitality that necessitates the abuse of one's family. While in the Hebrew tradition sacrifices were made as one means of sustaining a relationship with Yahweh, they were never intended to be a means of appeasing human recalcitrance in the face of injustice and violence. Moreover, there is every reason to believe that human sacrifice was not an acceptable part of Israelite tradition (e.g., Genesis 22; Mic 6:7b), and Lot's actions therefore are further attested as fulfillment of his own quest for favorable recognition of a violent community. As Tapp notes, the virgin daughters have been objectified, and made into non-events.[26]

A great part of the irony here is that Lot seeks to convince the men of Sodom not to act wickedly, yet he fails to recognize the wicked violence of his own actions In fact through his words he gives the men of Sodom carte blanche permission to act as violently as they wish against his daughters. While the Hebrew phrase "according to what is good/pleasing in your eyes" (*kaṭṭôb beʾenekem*) has become an idiom for doing that which is pleasing, in this context we hear an additional dimension. This offer by Lot to do that which is "pleasing" feels inherently related to "hurriedness" and haste. In a hasty way, as a hasty remedy to the possibility of violence, Lot offers his daughters. Clearly his actions are not well thought out, as is typically the case with "hurried" actions.

---

heroic. Sarna, *Genesis*, 135, also concludes that, "Lot is true to his code of honor. Hospitality was a sacred duty, according the guest the right of asylum." Luther, *Lectures on Genesis 15–20*, 259, also concludes, "I excuse Lot and think that he adopted this plan without sinning. He did not plan to expose his daughters to danger, for he knew they were not desired by the frenzied men; but he hoped that this would be a way to soften their wrath. Therefore this speech should be regarded as a hyperbole." See Skinner, *Genesis*, 307. Regarding Lot's actions, Skinner concludes that they show Lot, "as a courageous champion of the obligations of hospitality . . . and is recorded to his credit."

26. Tapp, "An Ideology of Expendability," 158.

He would not have recognized the violence of his daughters "serving" the desires of the men. The use of *kaṭṭôb beʾenekem* here is extraordinarily enlightening, for the men of Sodom have made it abundantly clear that they were entirely incapable of acting ethically. These men have already acted in terms of what they have determined to be good and right. Now Lot urges them in a new context to use their ubiquitously maladroit judgment in doing whatever pleases them against the virgin daughters. The best that might be said about Lot here is that he uses poor judgment.

The loss of innocence by the daughters cannot be underestimated, for even though the daughters are not physically abused by the men of Sodom, the damage is already done, for their innocence is destroyed. Indeed the very act of their father is a profound act of destroying their innocence. Consider the innocence that is destroyed in war. Even though a soldier may never be physically wounded, the reality of being in a theatre of war itself destroys the innocence of the person. Both war and rape involve far more than the physical act of violence; they both include at the core, the wounding, often irreparably, of the spirit.

Lot's address to the men as "my brothers" suggests a couple of things. First, Lot mistakenly assumes that having resided in Sodom he is able to identify with the Sodomites on a familial basis. They would, however, remind him that he was still considered very much a "sojourner" (*ger*). In their estimation, though the *ger* had certain rights, those rights did not include correcting their behavior.[27] Further, the Sodomites' hospitality to a *ger* did not include the right to make a self-determination of "belonging"; the Sodomites would set and determine the boundaries of those rights. In the eyes of the Sodomite men, if Lot were truly a "brother" he would not object to their request. After all the unity of the city and the uniformity of purpose is succinctly captured in v. 4. All the men are of one mind and unless Lot joins them, there is no way he could be a "brother."[28]

---

27. On the matter of the consequences of Lot being an outsider, see Brisman, *The Voice of Jacob*, 62: "The Sodomites attack Lot for setting himself up as judge of others—he who was just a visitor, a stranger, now lords it over them in moral judgment (19:9)."

28. Sarna, *Understanding Genesis*, 146, concludes: "It is clear from our story that Lot, in offering hospitality to the strangers had violated the norms of the society in which he lived, and the angry citizens soon came to give vent to their sense of outrage." One might note that the irony here is that Lot seeks to do what might be considered noble and meets with anger and rejection.

Second, it is an irony that Lot ingratiates himself with the men of Sodom as a way of establishing familial identity. The underlying hope here is that these men will act according to the standards appropriate for family members. The naiveté of Lot here is overwhelming. There is no mistaking the irony, for Lot who seeks a kinship with the men of Sodom is about to sacrifice brutally his own daughters!

Prevalent in this narrative is the rejection of the notion that familial ties should assure care and protection. While tradition dictates that in familial systems there is an inherent source of centralized power, the daughters are pushed from their inherent right as members of the center, to disposable objects of the margin. In the case of the virgin daughters, their father, the one family member who has been granted power by the society, treats them as a piece of meat easily discarded for the sake of appeasing the violent men of Sodom. As their father, Lot represents both the powerful and the powerless in their family. Using Judges 19 as a parallel here, the actions of Lot would be the equivalent of sentencing his daughters to a violent death. The strangers, not the family members demonstrate hospitality and care. It is the strangers who step in and save both Lot and his family. The strangers, whose very status places them at the margin, are the ones who act on behalf of both the dislocated (virgin daughters) and those who remain at the center.[29]

A reality of the city of Sodom is that it clearly has become something of an incestuous city. That is to say, outsiders were not welcome, so much so that violence is the result of their presence. With such an orientation, there is absolutely no toleration of outside advice and most certainly no interest in divine intervention.[30] The unity of purpose by all the men of the city testifies to this. Though bound together, they sought to separate themselves from all others. Those who would dare to

---

29. Cf. The Levite in Judges who refused to spend the night among "foreigners" and instead went to Gibeah, his "family members." There, no one invited him into their house except another sojourner. Instead, the men of Gibeah raped and killed his wife.

30. One is led to think here of Genesis 11 where the people sought to build a tower and thereby separate themselves. Like God's interest in seeing personally what was happening in Sodom, God would also come down and see what was happening in Babel. What God found was a city that was seeking to separate itself from everyone else and in the process become incestuous. Separation and sectarianism will not be tolerated. The circle must include both the center and the margin. Neither is able to function independently. Indeed, there cannot by its very nature be a center without a margin. The connection between the two is intrinsic. God would have none of it.

transgress the "law" of the land would meet with grave consequences.[31] Such attitudes and actions of the men of Sodom resembles modern day actions of the Nazis who sought to banish all strangers from their midst, in anticipation of establishing a nation of "pure" people. Even those who had lived among them for a lifetime, for all practical purposes, people of that land came under fire because of ethnic and religious ancestral ties.

The violent attack on the strangers and Lot goes far beyond a sexual issue. All the more troublesome is the fact that Lot totally misses the central issue. That which was morally acceptable was determined by the code shaped by the Sodomites, not by a universal standard allowing for the care of all people. Moreover, the comparison between Sodom and modern day movements that seek separation from certain sections of society, is further strengthened by the fact that hospitality to strangers was an oriental custom universally accepted and respected. The fact that all of the men of Sodom refused to abide by this custom demonstrates the ingrained nature to pursue an evil course. There is a force which has systemic or structural influence that arguably transcends the voice of the individual objector.

Hearing and Seeing the Outcry

The evil course exhibited by the men of Sodom, characterized the "outcry" of the city. The term "outcry" taken on the surface level fails to explicate fully the seriousness of the crimes committed. In part because of the generality which "outcry" implies, and the textual ambiguity with regard to "outcry," some have concluded incorrectly and inappropriately that the "outcry" in this text specifically refers to the homosexual attack on the visitors, when in truth, the outcry constitutes first and foremost a judgment on the insidious manner in which the people in Sodom treated each other. That is to say, the "outcry" of the city had to do fundamentally with internal crimes.

---

31. Note Brueggemann, *Genesis*, 99, who, commenting on Genesis 11, points out that there are two kinds of unity, the better of which, and the one willed by God, is "that all of humankind shall be in covenant with him (9:8–11) and with him only, responding to his purpose, relying on his life-giving power."

Other instances in which the term ṣeʿaqah (outcry) is used in the Hebrew Bible demonstrate vividly particular crimes and actions.[32] Three examples of different circumstances will aid in the understanding of the breadth of the term.

First, the anguished cry of those kept in bondage under an oppressive regime is heard by God (Exod 3:7) and consequently God acts on their behalf. When members of the created order groan, regardless of the circumstances, God hears and acts.[33] We find a second, contrasting example in Exod 22:21–23. In the midst of several social laws, the people are warned that the oppression of the weak in their midst will lead to action by Yahweh. The possibility of oppressing family members is sounded here, and the actions of God on their behalf will be no less devastating than that of the punishment meted out against the Egyptians. Third, in Gen 4:10, after Abel is murdered, Cain is satisfied that the evidence is gone: no one will discover his crime. Answering God, Cain snaps at God saying that he is not responsible for his brother. What is stunning about the use of ṣeʿaqah in Gen 4:10 is the fact that it is not uttered from the mouth of a person. Rather, the cry comes through the dramatic image of the very blood of the innocent. In the matter of oppression that leads to an outcry, no part of creation will be able to hide the signs alerting Yahweh.[34] Two passages further aid us in giving concreteness to the general "outcry."

Isaiah 5:8

The climactic verse to Isaiah's "Song of the Vineyard" captures in poetic form the radical departure from the expectations of Yahweh and the actions of the people.

> [Yahweh] expected justice (*mišpat*),
> but saw bloodshed (*mišpah*);
> righteousness (*ṣedaqah*),
> but heard a cry (*ṣeʿaqah*). (Isa 5:7b)

---

32. See Jer 23:14, where Sodom and Gomorrah are associated with specific acts of wrongdoing.

33. See Fretheim, *Exodus*, 60.

34. Wilbur's refrain "And Ev'ry stone shall cry," in the hymn, "A Stable Lamp is Lighted," announcing the birth of the Messiah sounds this notion of creation, crying out even if the human voice is silent.

Instead of the expected *mišpat*, Yahweh found *mišpaḥ*, and instead of *ṣᵉdaqah*, *ṣᵉʿaqah* was prevalent. The message of the prophet is encapsulated in the contrasting scenarios of these four words.

Isaiah 5:1–6 establishes clearly the reality that the expectations of Yahweh are borne out of the prior actions of Yahweh on behalf of creation.[35] The creation motif in this text reminds the reader that matters of justice and righteousness are rooted in the very creation of a people. These are the fundamental responses that must be given by the people. Justice and righteousness are the pillars which characterize Yahweh's expectations within the community and the relationship amongst the people. It is the absence of *mišpat* and *ṣᵉdaqah* that lead to "outcry." Fundamentally, these terms have to do with relationship, both with divine and human relationships. The prophet's culmination in Isa 5:7 with the perversion of *mišpat* and *ṣᵉdaqah* underline the dual breakdown of the relationship. What then constitutes the change from *mišpat* to *mišpaḥ*, and *ṣᵉdaqah* to *ṣᵉʿaqah*? Particularly in Isa 5:8, we have a clear outline of the nature of this specific injustice: economic injustice. This, however, is not some kind of clinical economic endeavor void of relationship qualities.[36] The reality here is that members of the covenant community have begun to treat the land as a possession to trade and secure for themselves. In so doing, they have not only accumulated vast amounts of land, but summarily have crushed and virtually destroyed the very people with whom they have a covenantal relationship. Indeed, this very land represents the basis of the relationship as established and gifted by Yahweh. The usurpation of the land, which they illegally encroach upon, and exercise authority over, is not theirs. This action represents a flagrant flaunting in the face of Yahweh. The issue of community cannot be overlooked here, for these people have been called into community and their existence is tied to this kind of relationship. The outcry against the injustice points to the fact that oppressed members of the community who therein should rightfully gain their identity

---

35. For an extensive discussion of these terms, see Gossai, *Social Critique by Israel's Eighth-Century Prophets*; and Achtemeier, "Righteousness in the OT," 83.

36. Brueggemann, "Land, Fertility and Justice," draws an interesting and helpful connection between sexuality and economics in the Hebrew Bible. While he develops this parallel in a discussion of land issues, his remarks are germane to the present discussion. The promiscuity which prompts Lot to dispose of his daughters is tied to the domination of the land which one finds in Isa 5:8. The expression might be different, but the outcry against injustice is the same.

and strength, have been made to dwell by themselves. Because of this, Yahweh will act accordingly, and those who are the oppressors will be disallowed from dwelling in the luxurious homes; the land which they have taken away from the poor will not bring about the kinds of yields that they expect (Isa 5:8).

What is clearly evident in the select texts is the fact that "outcry" has wide and varied meanings associated with it. Rather than implying one particular crime, the outcry in Sodom suggests a veritable plethora of evil present.[37] $Ṣ^{e\text{c}}aqah$ is used exclusively with reference to human distress, and along with this is the action by Yahweh. Where there is an outcry, Yahweh hears and acts. While in the bondage situation in Egypt, God acts on behalf of the Hebrews: a people about to be born; in the case of the destruction of Sodom, God acts simply because of the internal decay and chaos of the society. The attack on Lot and the strangers, together with Lot's offer of his daughters reflect the breakdown of the order and moral fiber of the society. Moreover, it is to be noted that God's actions against Sodom is predicated on a code of conduct expected of all people, whether it is the systemic action against individual strangers or nation against nation.

Isaiah 1:10–17

The prophet's reference to Sodom and Gomorrah in this text in speaking to Judah's sinful ways, catalogues the multitude of elements which constitute sinfulness. That Judah is compared to Sodom and Gomorrah, not only points to the degree of Judah's condition, but provides some evidence of the nature and extent of the outcry recorded in Sodom in Genesis 18. Fundamentally, the prophet reprimands the people for substituting extravagant ritual propriety for social consciousness and matters of justice.

The ire of Yahweh is set alight by the extent of the people's blatant disregard to the impoverished state of other covenant members. Even though there is no pronouncement of total destruction in this text, the

---

37. See Ezek 16:49–50 where the prophet makes it abundantly clear that the "outcry" must not be interpreted in a narrow sense. It is the creation of a marginalized community of those with whom one is related, and the subsequent diminishing of their existence. The matter at hand is fundamentally a lack of care of the oppressed in a variety of ways.

gravity of Yahweh's responses is self-evident, as shown by the extremity of the severed relationship (v. 15). Continued active communication under all circumstances is a necessary component of a healthy relationship and partnership between believers and the God in whom they trust. The breakdown of the communication through a variety of expressions, signals a broken a relationship. The relentless voice of the believer, in joy and praise or in distress (e.g., Pss 88, 100) heard by the caring compassionate ear of God, sustains the relationship and maintains mutual confidence in each other. The relationship between the human and the divine is fostered not only on the basis of actions, but also on the continued proper tension between speaking and hearing.[38]

One is able to conclude therefore, that in v. 15, both of the necessary elements for God's response to human petitions will be discontinued: God will neither "see" nor "hear." Humans gauge the extremity of this pronouncement from the belief that seeing and hearing are essential for a proper relationship. The punishment here is to be construed, at one level, as the end of all communication, hence the termination of the relationship. God executes devastating, though not final action.

The distancing in the relationship is captured in the words, "your hands are full of blood" (v. 15c). The hands, a traditional part of the ritual of prayer, are the same hands that are stained with the blood of the neighbor. Hence Yahweh closes the eyes and ears to the prayers of the people who come with blood-stained hands.

Yet, rejection is not the last word by Yahweh. It is clear that it is unacceptable to have the blood of any human being on one's hands and this fact is further heightened when associated with the blood of one's kin. Though not an insurmountable obstacle (Isa 1:10), blood on the hands most certainly stands in the way of what would be a proper relationship, either refracting or voiding care and hospitality. The spilling of one's blood results from expressions of hostility. Because of the modern connotation of hostility, often there is a tendency to overlook the more subtle forms of hostility. Hostility might very well manifest itself in a form that is so subtle that it goes unrecognized by the source.

---

38. Note the temple sermon in Jeremiah 7, where the critical framework of speaking and listening is broken by the people, and thus the divine human relationship is fractured. Also, Fretheim, "Prayer," who maintains that prayer is the primary mode of communication between humanity and God, and when this is absent or strained then the relationship is vulnerable.

Thus, in ancient Israel, there were those who secured the estates of the smaller landowners under the guise of economic enterprise and legitimate entrepreneurship (e.g., Isa 5:8; Amos 8:4). We see evidence of the incongruous nature of this life style, as the rich landowners continued to participate in the activities of the cult, undaunted by their actions against members of the covenant community. These members of the covenant community, are oblivious to the intrinsic connection between economics and cultic activity.

The unbreakable progression of nine imperatives in vv. 16–17 establish that which is necessary for restoration. The cleansing of oneself is not merely a matter of ritual purity, but as we read in Isa 1:16, this cleansing has an intrinsic connection to social justice. This understanding of "washing" departs radically from the tradition. The washing of blood-stained hands cannot be camouflaged by ritual propriety and cultic regularity.

Lot: On Choosing Death

In vv. 12ff., the identity of the visitors has been revealed and they give Lot the opportunity to save himself, and indeed invite him to save the members of his family. Lot must decide who is to be saved. Despite all the actions of Lot that have been less then laudable in matters of life and death, God offers him the opportunity to pursue life. We recall that according to the bartering between Abraham and Yahweh, there were less than ten righteous to be found in Sodom. At this point, it is evident that human righteousness is not humanly created or earned. Lot becomes much more of a case study in this regard, rather than a particular reflection of individual righteousness. The fact of the matter is that Lot's violent and totally despicable act of offering his daughters to be raped, makes it abundantly clear that his "righteousness" is not induced by his actions. Righteousness here and indeed elsewhere in the narrative is a gift from Yahweh.

The seriousness of the situation in Sodom and the inherent violent nature of Lot's actions are never fully comprehended by Lot. The lack of urgency which characterized Lot's actions towards the strangers in the opening scene (9:1–3) again come to bear as he responds to the visitors' urgent questions in 19:12. The narrator continues to focus on Lot as the one who needs to make critical decisions that will lead to life. At the point where the visitors admonish him to save his family, Lot is further remiss in his sense of immanent danger. His ineffectual behavior stands in sharp contrast to the life and death scenario that confronts him.

The visitors are certainly aware of the members of Lot's family; surely the ones who were present in the house. Thus, ignorance does not prompt the question in 19:12, but rather the visitors offer Lot yet another opportunity to redeem himself. Redemption at this point of the story is essential for Lot, as he is the one who sold, perhaps worse yet, gave away his daughters ostensibly in order to uphold the hospitality tradition. Indeed one might venture to say, that Lot bought himself out of what was evidently a situation of death, by the giving away of his daughters. In effect, he did what was precisely the opposite of redemption. With the visitors' urging, Lot has the chance of "buying back" the lives of his daughters and the rest of the family. This is an invitation to pursue life. To this point, there is no evidence that Lot is consciously aware of the tensions in the life and death scenario and the fact that he has consistently chosen death. Destruction of Sodom is immanent, and this conclusion to destroy has been reached through "seeing the outcry" in the city. The Hebrew phrase, *penê 'adonai* (19:13) is to be understood in the light of 18:21. It is the face-to-face encounter between Yahweh and the evil Sodom that finally brought about the decision to destroy.

Lot's inability to grasp the gravity of the visitors' admonition is further attested by the fact that apparently he does not tell his wife and daughters of the immanent danger, and in all likelihood does not urge them. Certainly there is no sign in his previous actions that there was a sense of urgency. Instead he leaves the house and relays the message to his prospective sons-in-law.[39] That the sons-in-law respond in disbelief might suggest three conclusions.

First, it is possible that the sons-in-law are unaware of the events that transpired earlier in the evening. One might be led to this conclusion as we are told that Lot "went out" to his sons-in-law. The fact that they were not a part of his household at the time, might incline one to conclude that they were unaware of the grand uproar. If this is the case, then Lot would again be delinquent in his responsibility to inform his sons-in-law. They were in all likelihood engaged to his daughters,

---

39. Jeansonne, *The Women of Genesis*, 38, suggests that *hatan* used in this context could be properly translated "future sons-in-law," thereby maintaining the fact that the daughters were virgins.

and must surely have some sense of what had taken place. There is no indication that Lot told them and consequently, the call to leave Sodom was not taken with seriousness.

Second, it might be concluded that, as Lot spoke, a casual tone of voice or his words allowed the sons-in-law to dismiss the threat of destruction. This, coupled with the possibility that the sons-in-law were unaware of the "outcry" in the city might have led them to dismiss the seriousness of Lot's call. Moreover, we assume that the sons-in-law were no strangers to Lot. They must have been familiar with his mannerisms; hence their response is particularly troublesome, for it reflects that Lot was fundamentally one who did not have credibility.[40]

Third, the narrator might be hyperbolic in the assessment of the level of participation of the men of Sodom, but this notwithstanding, it raises questions about the nature of the sons-in-laws. If indeed *all* the men of Sodom (19:4) were involved in the violence against the household of Lot and the visitors, then one would have to conclude that the sons-in-law would be a part of this affront. All the circumstantial evidence in the text lead the reader to conclude that the sons-in-law must have been aware of the city-wide gathering at Lot's house. It would indeed be an extraordinary matter for them to have remained unaware of the violence that was taking place in the city. Moreover, the intentional ambiguity in the text casts a shadow of doubt in the minds of the readers with regard to the sons-in-law. Their lack of any serious attention to the message of Lot may hold another dimension: with abject cynicism, they may doubt the power and probability of Yahweh to destroy Sodom. Likely also, is the fact that they reflected the arrogance of Sodom. Lot's journey to the sons-in-law is described only as "Lot went out" which is precisely the same description we have in 19:6 where Lot "went out" to the men of the city to reason with them about abusing his guests. There is no intimation that Lot went to a different house to meet with his sons-in-law and if indeed the sons-in-law were involved in the violence against Lot and the household, then they would have been struck blind by the visitors also. That they do not come with Lot and leave the city might reflect their obstinacy, or may serve as a point of reference for the destruction of all of the people of Sodom. Even in the face of death,

---

40. See Coats, "Lot," 123, who notes that the Hebrew participle in v. 14 used by the sons-in-law to describe Lot is *kimṣaḥeq*, the verbal root of which has to do with laughing. Thus Lot might be described as a laughingstock.

the sons-in-law refuse to believe and thus choose to die with all others. There is simply not enough evidence to determine conclusively whether or not the sons-in-law participated as the group surrounded the house of Lot, but an adequate number of ambiguities and overtones suggest that they were not entirely divorced from the proceedings.

One final note about this matter. If the sons-in-law were indeed blinded along with the other men of Sodom, then Lot's actions in seeking to convince them might either be construed as noble in the face of unavoidable destruction, or yet another example of his inability to discern the nature of the happenings and the urgency of the situation. As with Lot, one is wont to question, even challenge the ability of the sons-in-law to perceive what is evil and what is good.

Lot's inability to fathom the gravity of the whole situation is further amplified by the fact that in the morning the guests have to urge Lot to leave Sodom with his wife and daughters (19:15). That the visitors are the ones to coerce Lot into seeking life underlines the lack of urgency demonstrated by Lot.[41] The reluctance of Lot's wife to leave Sodom does not in any way reflect a condoning of the behavior that she witnessed just the night before. Rather, she recognizes the radical re-shaping of one's identity that a move such as this would make.[42] Looking back reflects a moment of sadness as she severs a relationship. This is an act of displacement and while we are aware that leaving Sodom will bring life, it is also a movement from center to margin for Lot and his family. Landlessness is one of the quintessential expressions of marginality and now Lot's family will face this reality. Of note however, is the potential for life even in a state of marginality as seen through the invitation of the angels. Lot's future and that of his family will have to be borne out of a nomadic existence. Lot, who to this point has not demonstrated any sense of urgency, is allowed to live and the only actions that might be vaguely called dallying, results in her death.[43]

---

41. Cf. Brisman, *The Voice of Jacob*, 62, who advances the notion that, "When Lot tries to persuade his sons-in-law, they regard him as *kimṣaḥeq*—'as one who jests,' as a Yitzchak, an Isaac. (19:14) Lot may not be successful in addressing them with prophetic voice, any more than he was successful in addressing the Sodomites the night before in protest against their sexual designs on his guests. But Lot does not hesitate to make his voice heard." Brisman might be allowing Lot more credit than he deserves at this point!

42. See, e.g., Ruth 1:16ff., which aids in the definition of the elements that give shape to a person's identity. The leaving behind of one's home is not an unimportant matter in one's life.

43. Jeansonne, *The Women of Genesis*, 39, suggests that in all likelihood it is Lot's

The reality of the daughters' fate is further exemplified through Lot's decision to spend the evening with the prospective sons-in-laws. This action confirms yet again that the daughters are about to be sacrificed and are in fact deemed expendable within the framework of the fate of Lot and Sodom. Lot's procrastination not only jeopardizes the lives of the three women, but his actions build on the intent of the narrator. Lot's action in 19:15–22 are in sharp contrast to that of the guests in these same verses. Lot is urged (v. 15),[44] but he lingers (v. 16). He is told to flee (v. 17 [2x]) and hurry (v. 22), but instead of seeking life for the members of his family, he negotiates for his personal gain.[45]

A Daring Choice for Life

The daughters of Lot function as a counterpoint specifically to Lot and Abraham and to the patrilineal tradition in Genesis. While Lot and Abraham are willing to sacrifice the future for the sake of the present, the daughters sacrifice the present in two ways. First, the assurance and security of their father is relinquished as they have a sexual encounter with him. Given the fact that the narrator suggests that Lot and the daughters were isolated, the daughters' sacrifice is not to be overlooked. Second, the moral and legal code of the society prohibited incestuous relations, and the daughters in the face of this prohibition, sought a future.

---

negligence in relaying the angels' message to his wife that led to her reluctance to leave and her death.

44. The Hebrew term used here for the urging of Lot is *vayya'iṣu*, and has a different connotation from *pṣr* as is used by Lot in 19:3. The connotation in 19:15 suggests that in the face of the immanent danger, Lot is "sitting around" and there is no sign of movement on his part. See, e.g., Josh 10:13 where the sun did not set, but "stood still" (*'md*).

45. The Hebrew term used in 19:16 to express Lot's dallying is the hithpael of *mahah*. To understand and appreciate the extent of Lot's lingering, the usage of *mahah* in two other contexts is instructive. In Isa 29:9, the hithpael form of *mahah* is rendered "stupefy," denoting a state of being in which a person is incapable of acting judiciously. This sort of action endangered the person and circumvented the opportunity for newness. A second use of *mahah* is found in Exod 12:39. In this context, the matter of life and death choices clearly gives definition to the message of the text. To be sure, it is the haste and urgency of the retreat from Egyptian bondage that precipitated the need for unleavened bread, but perhaps more importantly, lingering would have dire consequences, with death as a likely outcome. It seems that the combination of a state of stupification, and lack of awareness of life and death issues, lead Lot to act in the manner in which he did. Lingering on his part is an invitation to death.

Moreover, the patrilineal line in Genesis leaves no doubt as to the subsumed role of women. Among the categories of oppressed or absent women, is that of daughters. Whether it is the sons of Adam and Eve; the sons of Noah; the sons of Abraham and Sarah; the sons of Jacob and Rachel, the presence and desirability of sons over daughters is clearly a dominant motif in Genesis. In light of this preponderance, the action of the daughters must be noted, both for its own sake, and for the irony that it generates through the birth of two sons!

Immediately, one notes the daughters' decisive action (v. 31). This portrayal offers a rich contrast to Lot's indeterminacy and serves to underline Lot's delinquency.

A further example in the narrator's interest in underlining Lot's delinquency is spelled out in contrast between Lot and his daughters. When the daughters realize that not only has Sodom been destroyed, but that their very future was in danger of being annihilated, they acted with immediacy and urgency. They have no guide, save their own sense of what is essential for their future. According to society, their lives have reached a dead end; yet they make a daring decision. We know that after the death of Lot's wife, Lot and the two daughters are alone (19:30). The very absence of the sons-in-law and the prospect of an abrupt ending to life prompt the daughters to take matters into their own hands.

While Lot had ignored the warnings of the guests and lingered in the face of destruction and death, the daughters face an even graver situation, and immediately make a radical and daring choice for life. Note two ironies here.[46]

First, the irony in the action of the daughters is that they undertake an act, noted and accepted as extremely violent. However, the consequences of the action of the daughters are not for their own pleasure or for that matter for their personal fulfillment, but for the larger purpose of continued life. Lot had sacrificed his daughters to a violent fate, for a culturally noble cause, namely hospitality at all costs. In doing what he did, he unwittingly chose death instead of life.

Second in Lot's intoxicated state, his daughters have sexual intercourse with him, unknown to him. As is noted earlier, one of the meanings associated with the term *mahah* is "stupefy," and here surely

---

46. For a working definition of irony as intended here, see Muecke, *The Compass of Irony*, 29: "The first formal requirements of irony are that there should be a confrontation or juxtaposition of contradictory, incongruous, or otherwise incompatible elements . . . But we need more than this—we need ironic intention."

this connotation might be associated with Lot's state. He is certainly mentally and physically incapable of making any kind of intelligent discernment.[47] Whether the stupification is created by wine, or is constitutive of a constant state of tardiness, the fact remains, life must be chosen and seized, when the occasion demands it. Lot failed; the daughters do not.[48] It seems to me that the actions of the daughters, taken outside of the biblical context, indeed, are to be condemned; yet, within the context of seeking new life for creation, in its very perverse complexity their actions are noble. Their actions must be understood in the light of their purpose to preserve an offspring and thus continue the possibility of life (19:34). There is simply nothing in the actions of the daughters that suggest that they act out of a moral deficiency.[49]

The narrative makes it clear that the daughters have not acted in any way that would question their reputation morally. At the time they were wantonly handed over to the men of Sodom, they were virgins. They were not women who sought to have sexual experiences entirely for their own pleasures, but rather, as they approached their father, they acted out of a care for future generations. The reality is that their actions, as daring and controversial as they may be, are an integral part of the creation promise to populate the earth. The flood narrative (Gen 7:1ff.) where in the midst of destruction is the meticulous concern for the continuation of life, parallels the actions of the daughters. The Lot tradition like the Noah tradition suggests that Lot and the daughters are the sole survivors in this region of the cataclysmic destruction.[50] It must be understood that whether it is an action such as the one of

47. Coats, "Lot," 125, further identifies this irony when he observes that, "Lot, the passive fool, becomes the father of two sons, indeed of two nations without taking the initiative."

48. Some scholars have argued that the daughters' behavior under any circumstances is reprehensible and must be disapproved of. Alexander, "Lot's Hospitality," 291, concludes that, "Lot is the victim rather the instigator of this disgraceful affair." Also Dillman, *Genesis*.

49. Westermann, *Genesis 12–36*, 315, correctly observes that, "central is the primeval motif of the rising again of new life or of a new generation after an annihilation. This can take a great variety of narrative forms. Here it takes the form of a desperate act of two young women whose sole concern is to acquire posterity so that the family may live on."

50. Rosenberg, *King and Kin*, 76, points out that the Sodom story is, "rich in associations that reach out through the cycle and beyond, both backward (to the Garden story, the Flood and Babel) and forward (to other episodes of disasters among foreign peoples such as Genesis 34, Exodus 4–15 and Joshua 6)."

Lot's daughters, or the action of Tamar (Genesis 38), the intent of the narrator is not to create paradigms, but rather to exhibit in extreme particularities, the extent to which life is sought and preserved.

The provision for life after destruction is connected to the pain that this type of destruction and death cause Yahweh. It is always the overarching intent of God to preserve life, both for Israel and others (e.g., Gen 3:21; 22:33; Jon 3:10).[51] The fact that Lot is preserved from destruction in no way reflects Lot's righteousness.[52] Rather, Lot is, in a sense, paradigmatic of those who are within the boundaries of God's saving grace.[53]

---

51. Brueggemann, *Genesis*, 173, notes that the Hebrew term *hapak*, rendered "recoil" in Hos 11:8, implying that the heart of God is ripping apart, is also used in Gen 19:21, 25, 29. He suggests that God has taken the destruction and the pain of the people personally. To be sure, the crimes of the city are taken seriously, but God does not relish the destruction of a people. The parent-child motif is useful in aiding us in understanding the perspective of a God who is deeply pained, even as God is the one who punishes. The intrinsic relationship between God and all created order is captured repeatedly in the biblical material. See, e.g., Hos 11:1ff. and Jer 31:20, which capture the tension in the heart of God.

Also Fretheim, who, commenting on God's hearing of the people's cry says, "For God to 'know' the people, testifies to God's *experience* of this suffering, indeed God's *intimate* experience. God is here depicted as one who is intimately involved in the suffering of the people. God has so entered into their suffering as to have deeply felt what they are about to endure. God has chosen not to remain safe and secure in some heavenly abode, untouched by the sorrows of this world" (*Exodus*, 60).

The common strain that unites both the Exodus moment and the Hosea reference is the fact that Israel, God's chosen is the recipient of this intimate relation. What is remarkable about the use of *hapak* in the Sodom narrative is precisely the fact that this is a reference to God's pain even on behalf of "outsiders." The creation motif in this narrative cannot be overlooked.

52. Contra Turner, *Announcements of Plot in Genesis*, 82, who speculates that, "Lot's rescue could only be seen as a further example of Lot's crucial importance to the fulfillment of the promise—how else could one view the preferential treatment extended to him?" In contrast to Turner's view, see, Marks, "The Book of Genesis," 13, who concludes, "significant is the virtual elimination of Lot as recipient of the divine promise."

53. See Coats, *Genesis*, 101, who concludes that Lot is no more than a foil in this narrative: "The Lot tradition sets out a comic contrast with the man of faith, not as a competitor, not as an example of the man of unfaith, but as a comic-tragic buffoon." That some of Lot's actions might be comical perhaps remain uncontestable in some circles. However, the critical nature of the situation forces one to conclude that Lot was anything but comic. Lot's actions can only be perceived to be advocating violence and death. There is nothing comical about these matters.

4

Risking the Future for the Present

Genesis 20

AS WE READ THE THREE WIFE-SISTER EPISODES IN GENESIS (GEN 12:10–20; 20:1–18; 26:1–11), we note common elements that unite all three.[1] No scholarly consensus exists regarding the origin of the earliest strand, and indeed the premise of this discussion does not depend on such a consensus.[2] While the form-critical and source-critical studies of this text are diachronic in approach, the present undertaking is synchronic. The choice of Genesis 20 for the present study with its more complete and complex development of themes, rests on the nature and presentation of theological and moral dilemmas, either underdeveloped, or all together absent from the other two accounts.[3]

Though Abraham has scarcely begun his appointed journey, major challenges continually confront him. These issues are not peripheral, but rather they are issues that demand resolution, thus ensuring the

---

1. For a form-critical study of these three stories, see, Koch, *The Growth of the Biblical Tradition*, 111–32.

2. Van Seters suggests that of the three accounts, Genesis 12 might have been the earliest, though Genesis 20 appears to have been the most developed. For a discussion and comparison of these three accounts, see *Abraham in History and Tradition*, 167ff. Also Koch, having done extensive form-critical work on the these three versions, concludes that, "Crudely stated, A is the most ancient, B the middle version and C the most recent of the story." *The Growth of the Biblical Tradition*, 125. For a different view, see Noth, *A History of Pentateuchal Traditions*, 102ff. Noth sees the Isaac cycle in Genesis 26 as the original. For a helpful critique of Koch, and a brief, but useful survey of the range of methodological positions that have been proffered, see Niditch, *Underdogs and Tricksters*.

3. Rosenberg, *King and Kin*, 78, argues for the more elaborate nature of the second account in comparison to the first.

continuation of the journey. Though Abraham is aware of the reputation of Gerar and the wickedness associated with it, the narrator offers no reason for the stop-over at Gerar. Contrast such narrative silence with the specific explication in the Genesis 12 account, where we are told of the need to embark on the dangerous trip to Egypt. That dangerous trip to Egypt was necessary because of Abraham's overarching concern for life, for finding sustenance during a severe famine. Even though the encounter with Pharaoh cannot be ascribed fully to the need for survival, nevertheless there is the initial legitimate reason that sends him into Egypt.[4] In any event, his decision to go to Gerar with Sarah, creates critical questions.[5] It seems clear that such an act would endanger the promise, through the endangering of the ancestress Sarah: Abraham evinces a lack of trust as his actions demonstrate the priority of his personal protection takes precedence over elements of the promise and his actions express a magnified fear of foreigners.[6] While it might be said that Gerar cannot be trusted in light of its history, Abraham, by his actions, not only prevents a demonstration of hospitality by the Gerarites, but simultaneously contravenes one important component of the divine promise, namely that he would be a blessing to all people (Gen 12:3).[7] Moreover, Abraham is one who is charged explicitly to do justice and righteousness, both for himself and his descendants, for the ful-

---

4. Turner, *Announcements of Plot in Genesis*, 83–84, suggests that in Genesis 12, Abraham, "was morally accountable for the maltreatment of his wife, but at least he could argue that he was doing his best to preserve the promise. In Genesis 20 he is again morally culpable, but can no longer argue that his actions serve the divine purpose."

5. Miscall, "Literary Unity in Old Testament Narrative," 33, observes that, "The lack of regard for the wife is most serious in Genesis 20 because of its preceding context. Abraham because of his experience in Egypt, must be well aware of his nearly inevitable result of his lie . . ."

6. Patrick, *The Rendering of God in the Old Testament*, 81, notes that, "The background tension of the story is the vulnerability of foreigners in a strange land, particularly if they have something or someone desirable. The patriarch tries to neutralize the danger, but he actually aggravates it." Patrick's observation might very well be reversed and have a greater and more accurate impact on the story. While Sarah and Abraham are the foreigners in the story, it is Abimelech as the foreigner who is in danger because of Abraham's actions.

7. See, Coats, "A Threat to the Host"; he rightly emphasizes the blessing/curse matrix as a central component to the three versions of the story. Also, Biddle, "The 'Endangered Ancestress,'" 609: "Genesis 20 adds an account of Abimelech's graciousness toward the patriarch as evidence of his recognition that the patriarch can be the source of blessing for him."

fillment of the promise (Gen 18:19). As the story develops, it becomes clear that Abraham's actions have the potential to bring curse rather than blessing.

A further issue at stake in the encounter between Abraham and Abimelech is the clash between the powerful and the powerless. One certain expression of power is citizenship/ownership of a land. An established recognition for ages gone by and contemporaneously operative whether in the continuing struggles for identity in the Middle East today, or the newly found expressions of freedom in Eastern Europe, the issue is always finally the rightness of ownership or presence in a land; surely therein lies power. Being the king and citizen of Gerar established Abimelech as one with power. In terms of what gauges terrestrial power, there is no doubt that Abraham would be classified as powerless: he is without land! With this in mind, one can argue that Abraham sought to challenge the imperial power with human ingenuity and a manipulative ruse. Landlessness (insecurity) and the status of stranger might therefore be understood as the force behind the action of Abraham. This understanding of power is inverted as the narrative concludes, for it is Abraham who is guaranteed a status as one with power to give life, while Abimelech is made powerless and dependent.

Three conclusions might be drawn here. First, the power/powerless dichotomy is recast in terms of divine calling and intervention. Clearly, power gifted by the divine is reckoned not only in terms of wealth and political status, but also as mediator and restorer of life. Second, divine intervention cannot/must not be overlooked in one's state of powerlessness. Consequently, even though Abraham perceived the future in Gerar to be dangerous and fearful, his actions cannot finally be justified. Third, the narrative establishes not only the impotence of imperial power, but the impossibility that imperial power will shape the destiny of the divine promise, and further, the inevitable subservience of imperial to divine power (John 18:36ff.).

Abraham was given the mandate to bring new life and in the face of the childlessness and landlessness that he and Sarah experienced, the promise from Yahweh was designed to create a radical new beginning. In Gen 13:1, we are told that together with Sarah and Lot his nephew Abraham departed. Setting out together, Lot and Abraham soon head in separate directions; this would be a permanent separation. From here on, Abraham and Sarah would journey together, bearers of the promise. If there were any inkling that Lot would enter into the picture as the "promised descendant," his departure would bring to an end this hope and speculation. It is precisely this realization that comes to bear on the decisions of Abraham as he seeks to pawn Sarah off as his sister. As Sarah is identified as his sister, the nature of the familial relationship not only changes, but in fact the promise is placed in jeopardy.[8] For Abraham who is entrusted with the opportunity for new life has taken it upon himself to disassemble systematically the components of the promise, and it seems at one level that he is embarking on the road to death, rather than life. At this point in the pilgrimage, it is difficulty to be hopeful for the future, except for the constant reminders of who the promise maker is: Yahweh. In the face of what Abraham recognizes as "death," Abraham chooses to live a lie and estrange himself from Sarah and alienate himself from the foreigners of Gerar. Indeed, Rosenberg suggests that this episode is one, "in which the question of foreignness, as such, is most at issue."[9] For a journey that is designed with an eye for life in the future, it seems that Abraham was proceeding with an eye towards death.

While never mentioned explicitly in Genesis 20, the hidden issue in the episode is the endangering of the promised son.[10] But, more than this, Abraham's actions not only jeopardizes the chance for a son, but the chance for a future. The relationship between Abraham and foreigners sharply focuses the frailty of Abraham's faith and the persistent nature of God's grace. Abraham himself had demonstrated what hospitality was all about when strangers came to his door (Genesis 18) and he attended to them in extravagant fashion. They allowed him to function as a host or hostess should, without seeking to pre-empt his actions. Abraham however does not allow Abimelech and the people of Gerar to demonstrate such hospitality to him and Sarah. Rather, fear and distrust constitute his entire attitude. Consequently, in juxtaposition to Yahweh's overarching intention for reconciliation and restoration, the

---

8. Some scholars have argued that *kaʿet hayyah* in Gen 18:10 carries the meaning of being pregnant, and thus Abraham's pawning off of Sarah as his sister, literally pawns off the heir, in addition to Sarah. See, e.g., Clines, "The Ancestor In Danger."

9. Rosenberg, *King and Kin*, 77.

10. Contra Coats, "A Threat to the Host," 77, who suggests, "At no point in the development of the story is the issue that of Abraham's progeny or God's promise for progeny."

focus of the encounter with the people of Gerar is not on reconciliation and life, but on separation and death.[11] Fear paralyzed Abraham to the extent that he acted defensively and negatively.[12]

Distrusting the Promise

While it is true that Abraham might have had valid reasons to be wary of Gerar and Egypt (Gen 13:10), he is clearly motivated not by the promise and the components of the promise, but by fear and an overarching concern for the present reality and not for the future. Throughout this episode, one is struck by the irony in Abraham's actions. For one who is to be pre-eminently concerned about the future, Abraham is obsessed about the present. Considering the narrative emphasis on the future, Hugh White observes that, "This is a new mode of behavior for a Biblical personage and one that is consistent with the change that has occurred in Gen 12:1–3, that is, he now lives out of his anticipation of the future."[13] While White's observation is to the point, it is not the future shaped by the promise that occupies Abraham's attention, but a future shaped by fear and distrust. Motivated by fear in his preemptive stance against both Pharaoh and Abimelech, Abraham seeks to ensure that the present state of being is maintained at all costs. Fear as a design, then and now can only spell death; Abraham's decision to pawn Sarah off as his sister might appear to him to be an opportunity for him to

---

11. Niditch, *Underdogs and Tricksters*, 51, looking from a morphological perspective concludes, "The tale's interest ultimately is in the status quo; it ends in resolution, harmony and restoration; all is as it was. The disruption of a state of equilibrium is, in fact, the central problem of the tale." To the extent that Abraham and Sarah are united as husband and wife at the end of the narrative and broken relationships are again healed, Niditch is surely right in her conclusion. However, even given the ending of the narrative, it can hardly be called a reinstatement of the status quo. Things are the same and yet, they will never be the same again. In this regard, one thinks of Job and the restoration at the end of his ordeal. Things will never be the same for him.

12. See Nouwen, *The Wounded Healer*, 91, who suggests, "Hospitality is the virtue which allows us to break through the narrowness of our own fears and to open our houses to the stranger, with the intuition that salvation comes to us in the form of a tired traveler. Hospitality makes anxious disciples into powerful witnesses, makes suspicious owners into generous givers, and makes closed-minded sectarians into interested recipients of new ideas and insights." Using this insight from Nouwen one is led to conclude that not only did Abraham not act hospitably, but by his fear, he prevented Abimelech from being hospitable.

13. White, *Narration and Discourse in the Book of Genesis*, 179.

live, but in fact this action only signals death. In no way is his action noble. For a person who carries the promise, he selfishly thinks only of his personal welfare, disregarding the welfare of Sarah and their mutual commitment, not only as husband and wife, but as co-bearers of the promise. By saying that Sarah is his sister,[14] Abraham exhibits no trust in the promise-maker and the future as shaped by the promise-maker. While both Abraham and Sarah have embarked on a journey away from their home in order to follow the promise, it is apparent that Abraham has moved considerably away from the original plan. The language of *hithʿu* in v.13 suggests that Abraham has lost track of the original direction in which he embarked. Steinmetz concludes that with the use of *hithʿu*, the reader is clearly led to assume that Abraham has lost track of the destiny to which he is called.[15] It is the juxtaposition of Abraham's willingness to believe in the promise and exemplify himself as a person of faith (Gen 12:1–9) together with the fear and distrust that characterized his attitude to those persons whom he met along the way that give shape to this story. By not affording the people the opportunity to demonstrate their hospitality, Abraham jeopardizes the life of Sarah and the prospects of an heir, as Sarah, the one who would bear the son, becomes a member of the harem of Abimelech.

The fact that Abimelech takes Sarah unto himself might strike moderns as unethical in itself, and even in ancient times, it was not particularly acceptable. Yet, knowing fully that Sarah would be taken in by Abimelech, Abraham nevertheless goes ahead and identifies her as his sister.[16] Outside of Abraham's selfish action, the act by Abimelech

---

14. Speiser, *Genesis*, 89–94, argues that in pawning off Sarah as his sister, Abraham is following an old Hurrian practice, where not only could a wife be "transformed" into a sister, but in so doing she is raised to a higher level on the social ladder. Even if this historical connection were valid, however, it misses the theological and moral intent of the narrative and in any event does not excuse Abraham's decision. Sarna, *Understanding Genesis*, 102–3, also suggests that the "wife-sister" status endowed the woman with extra privileges. He argues that both Sarah and Rebekah came from societies in which the "wife-sister" tradition was established and acceptable. However, the transmission of this tradition into the patriarchal context raised a set of new questions.

15. Steinmetz, *From Father to Son*, 66.

16. See Gunkel, *The Legends of Genesis*, who argues that Abraham's action in pawning Sarah off as his sister was not only common at the time, but a "necessary lie" to save Abraham's life. He notes Jer 38:24ff as a parallel. Gunkel's argument appears untenable in the light of the larger issue at stake in Abraham's call. Moreover, Jeremiah's action recorded in 38:24–28 is hardly a parallel.

is despicable.[17] That the immediate action of a host to a guest in the land is to seek sexual relations at one level demonstrates inhospitality to Sarah. Yet, one can never be sure that this would have taken place had Abraham acted with integrity in the first place. Howsoever one looks at the situation, the action of Abraham had the potential for disaster.

Moreover, Abraham's actions suggest two possible directions. First, he sees his vision of the future as being on the same wavelength as that of Yahweh. This is surely one of the ongoing tensions in the narrative, as the actions of Abraham force us to struggle with determining the distinctions between human and divine vision. Implicit in Abraham's deportment is the belief that his perception of danger in the future, is the same as Yahweh's. While Abraham's decision to use Sarah as a foil might lead to the conclusion that Yahweh might have done the same given the vision of the future, there is more than ample evidence in the narrative that alternatives unknown to Abraham, were always available to Yahweh.[18] Such limited vision continues to be an eminently important matter for contemporary believers. In the face of seemingly insurmountable obstacles, and many expressions of suffering, human words and actions often imply insufficient and finite solutions. Yet, the biblical material indicates that human finitude must not be the measuring guide for divine action (cf. 1 Cor 13:12).

Second, Abraham exemplifies the notion that the human being is granted freedom to act independently of the divine, and this freedom in action is to reflect the wisdom and foresight of God. But did Abraham do this? Underlying this issue is a major theological contention regarding the extent of God's power. On the one hand, total dependence on Yahweh with no freedom for a proactive stance by Abraham, in effect would incapacitate Abraham rendering him passive. The result necessarily leads to a state of resignation. On the other hand, in taking matters

---

17. Westermann, *Genesis 12–36*, 322, notes that, "The abduction of a married woman was the violation of a divinely sanctioned ordinance." While this is true, it is not at all clear in this text that Sarah is abducted by Abimelech. Not only is there premeditation on the part of Abraham, but there is no indication that Sarah shows any great reluctance.

18. Westermann, *Genesis 12–36*, 167, commenting on Abraham's actions against Pharaoh, notes that, "Abraham sees no other way out than to surrender his wife. He has foreseen correctly that the surrender [of Sarah] can at least initially save the lives of both of them. Abraham was in fear of death; but the narrative continues to say throughout that there are further options open to God which Abraham does not see."

so completely into his own hands, Abraham would display an utter lack of confidence in and reliance on Yahweh as promise maker. In the light of the partnership motif that pervades the entire Abraham narrative, either of the above directions would prove to be inefficacious.

The narrative impels us to draw a parallel between the action of Lot in giving his daughters to the men of Sodom (Genesis 19) and the sacrifice of Sarah. Whether it is for the protection of the men in Genesis 19 or the protection of Abraham in the land of Gerar, the woman's life is endangered.[19] However, the issue at stake is even greater than the unprincipled actions of Abraham and Lot. Both Sarah and the daughters of Lot (Gen 19:31–38) are the ones who would be bearers of future generations. That is one of the critical issues in the narrative. To a certain extent, both Lot and Abraham are willing to sacrifice the future for the sake of the present. In light of the unknown length of the journey designed by the promise, and the reality that Abraham and Sarah are passing through Gerar, Abraham's calculations are myopic, sacrificing the future for the sake of the safety of the present. Moreover, both Abraham and Lot are aware of the immanent danger and vulnerability that the women will face, and yet there is no hesitancy on their part in sacrificing the woman.

The narrator in Genesis 20, unlike Genesis 12, does not provide many details of the happenings between Sarah and Abimelech. Indeed, Abraham does not consult Sarah on his intended plans for her temporary change of identity. But the intended result is the same as J's account in Genesis 12. Like Pharaoh's reaction, "And for her sake he dealt well with Abram" (Gen 12:16a). Abraham expected that Abimelech would deal well with him because of Sarah. These issues are very much a part of the Genesis 20 narrative, though the brevity with which they are addressed and the ambiguity that surrounds them, suggest that theological conclusions are not easy to construct.

The Outsider Pleads with Yahweh

In contrast to the brief announcements in 20:1–2, we note a more extensive development of the discourse and encounter between Abimelech

---

19. See Marmesh, "Anti-Covenant," 50, who observes that, "Sarah is the protector of Abraham at her own expense. In Genesis 26, Isaac repeats the exact pattern of his father."

and Yahweh in vv. 3–7.[20] The human-divine encounter in the biblical tradition is used again and again as a prelude for change, and often the encounter involves Yahweh and a believer such as the encounter with Jacob (Genesis 32), where Jacob is on his way to reconcile differences with Esau. Before the human reconciliation occurs, Jacob would first encounter the divine, and this experience equips him for the meeting with his brother. In a somewhat different vein, Job's encounter with Yahweh changes his understanding, both of his role as a human and the role and work of the divine (Job 42:5).

What is extraordinary about the encounter between Abimelech and Yahweh is the fact that Abimelech is an outsider, a foreigner.[21] As was the case with both Jacob and Job, Abimelech was facing death. Abimelech's encounter with Yahweh ushered in the news of his impending, yet not unavoidable death and the ensuing discourse with God provided a glimpse of hope for life. It is made immediately clear that it is divine not imperial power that will decide between matters of life and death. Abimelech recognizes this and proceeds on this basis in his discourse with Yahweh. It is certainly not an isolated instance here that life is bestowed even in the face of death. Jacob is reconciled with Esau; Job lives and begins a new life; Adam and Eve are allowed to live even though they ate of the forbidden fruit, the promised consequence of which was death. Through the encounter with the creator, each is given new life.

There is little subtlety in the narrator's interest in the encounter between Yahweh and the outsider, Abimelech. In the natural progression of the narrative, one would likely expect a conversation between Abraham and Yahweh. Yet, Abraham is never spoken to by Yahweh. This is the first of several examples of inversions in this narrative. About the time the reader expects Yahweh to speak with Abraham, it is Abimelech to whom the words of Yahweh are directed. This is the first instance in which the reader is alerted to the potential of the radical encounter. The presence and the role of the outsider in the journey of Abraham and Sarah cannot be overlooked. Far more significant in this episode is the conversation between Yahweh and the stranger. The question posed by

20. Viewing this encounter differently, Marmesh (ibid., 49–50) says, "The divine speaker confirms Abimelech's self-justification. The fact that Sarah was taken out of his house is completely dismissed by the complicity of the Lord and Abimelech."

21. Cf. the encounters between Yahweh and Hagar, the first of which was the stepping stone for Hagar's return to Sarah, and subsequent reconciliation, while the second involved blessing (Genesis 16, 21).

Abimelech; the "hearing" of Abimelech's words by Yahweh; the recognition by Yahweh of Abimelech's intent and the subsequent resolution allow Abimelech to pose critical questions to Abraham.

The mode of revelation is through a dream, again a manner through which Yahweh has spoken to others (e.g., Gen 31:24, where God speaks to Laban, also an outsider), and now speaks to Abimelech in similar fashion. The initial segment of the conversation is pointed and short. Abimelech is deemed responsible for having taken to himself a married woman, and for this prohibited action, the penalty is death. The pronouncement of death is made immediately in v. 3, prior to any discussion and is repeated again in v. 7, though in v. 7 the matter of death is linked to the fulfillment of the conditions outlined in the intervening verses. One might very well conclude that Abimelech and Yahweh discuss life and death issues. Abimelech might very well have asked Yahweh, "What might I do to live?" For Abimelech, it was truly a life and death situation.

Different levels of power are embodied by Yahweh and Abimelech. Clearly imperial power is relegated to a distant secondary tier in its negotiating leverage. Even with the power of the state, Abimelech's point of reference in the face of Yahweh is from the margin.

Even though the reference to the fact that Abimelech had not approached Sarah is likely a late addition to the narrative,[22] this does not detract from the importance of the statement. The Hebrew term *karab*, which is rendered "approach" in v. 4, certainly connotes sexual encounter, but also has an established biblical overtone of "hostility" (e.g., Pss 27:2; 68:3; Isa 8:3). The narrator seeks to establish that while the actions of Abimelech contravened the law of the people, it was not his intention to abuse Sarah, nor was there any premeditated hostility. Given the multi-faceted nature of *karab*, with references to war, hostility, sexuality, the narrator's comment on Abimelech is designed in large part to paint a picture of Sarah's experience with Abimelech as one not tainted by violence.

By the end of v. 3, the obvious conclusion that the reader draws is that Abimelech is the guilty one. It is, however, in v. 4 that Abimelech sets out to establish his innocence in the whole matter.[23] To be sure we are aware

---

22. Westermann, *Genesis 12–36*, 322, "The sentence has been added out of excessive caution."

23. See Carmichael, *Law and Narrative in the Bible*, 209: "Abimelech, king of Gerar,

at this point that it was Abraham who concocted the transformation of Sarah's relational status. However, it appears that Sarah has agreed to stand by Abraham's story. Thus, at this juncture Abimelech sees Sarah as an accessory in the entrapment.[24] Already it is evident that Abimelech has come to believe in the power and authority of Yahweh; if not, he would not have demonstrated any inclination towards the penitence that Abimelech shows. The discourse between Yahweh and Abimelech, with the general directions given to Abimelech assumes that he has understanding and discernment. It becomes clear from the imperative of Yahweh and the subsequent gifts of Abimelech to Abraham and Sarah, that the king certainly understood the nature of Yahweh's words. Moreover, his questioning of Yahweh's justice becomes the critical issue at this point, "Lord, will you destroy an innocent people?" (v. 4b). If indeed God is a just God, then God would not bring death on the innocent. The textual ambiguity surrounding, "innocent man" (NAB); "innocent or innocent ones"[25]; or "innocent people" (NRSV) provides some direction as to the larger consequence of the particular action of Abimelech. In the case of Abraham's plea on behalf of Sodom (Gen 18:22–33), the narrative in Genesis 18 suggests that it is not the particularity of Lot's presence in Sodom that prompts the query, yet grammatically *ṣaddiq ʿim-rašaʿ* is clearly singular. The fact that Abraham did not go beyond ten righteous Sodomites in the conversation with God indicates the use of *ṣaddiq ʿim-rašaʿ* as having larger public implications.

---

sought what he perceived to be a legitimate relationship with Abraham's sister, Sarah. She herself had let him think that she was free to become his wife." Also, Sternberg, *The Poetics of Biblical Narrative*, 315, who notes that for sixteen of the eighteen verses in the narrative, it is Abimelech who enjoys the role of the injured, the wronged, the sinned against party.

24. Carmichael, *Law and Narrative in the Bible*, 216, argues, "Nothing is said about the woman's involvement. Yet it is Sarah who encouraged the adulterous development because she deliberately concealed the fact of her marital status." While Carmichael's conclusion appears logical, we are cautioned that it was Abraham who as the patriarch, determined that Sarah act in this manner. Could Sarah have argued? Perhaps! Yet, it is precisely because she follows through willingly with the plan of Abraham that we are reminded of the nature of the patriarchal orientation and the fact that Sarah voice is stifled. Indeed, as if to accentuate Sarah's state of subservience and powerlessness, she is made to be silent throughout the entire Gerar episode. We have already witnessed (Hagar episodes) the lengths to which Sarah would go in order to ensure the fulfillment of the promise. In her defense one may argue that she was acting in this manner for the sake of the promise.

25. Westermann, *Genesis 21–36*, 322.

The issue at stake is the use of the particular to have universal ramifications. Likewise, Abimelech's pleading of his case cannot be understood solely on the basis of a personal exoneration. The action against Sarah has public overtones. Moreover, as king, Abimelech has the function of a corporate personality, and thus as he brings his case before Yahweh, he is not only pleading his own innocence, but also that of the people of Gerar.[26] Unlike Abraham who is an "insider" and Yahweh's promise-bearer, Abimelech has no such partnership or relationship with Yahweh. It is precisely the absence of Abimelech's identity in Yahweh that has this text reverberating with a creation motif and functioning beyond the establishment only for "insiders."[27] Yahweh is not the one on trial here, though Abimelech, knowing that Yahweh is the God of Abraham and Sarah, forces God to face the question of justice. Inherent in Abimelech's question, is the belief that God, being a just God, will not destroy an innocent people. Abimelech does not seek to establish any kind of superficial relationship with Yahweh. Rather, as creator-God, there is the expectation that God must act justly. To be sure, Abimelech presents a case, demonstrating his innocence and pointing to Sarah and Abraham as the guilty ones, but his question to Yahweh does not hinge either on his innocence or Abraham's guilt. Parallel to Abraham acting on behalf of Sodom (Genesis 18), Abimelech goes beyond the expected boundary, as an "outsider" seeks life under Yahweh's justice. Abimelech's recitation of the ritual formula, "I did this in the integrity of my heart and the innocence of my hand" (v. 5) drives home the plea of his innocence. Here, he is very much within the cultic tradition (Pss 24:4; 10:1–2).

The narrator's persistent emphasis on the dialogue between Yahweh and Abimelech further reinforces the fact that the focus is not on Abraham and his guilt, but on the justice of God and the manner in which God listens to, and acts on behalf of outsiders. Abimelech's plea of innocence and integrity does not go unnoticed and while it cannot

---

26. Steinmetz, *From Father to Son*, 70, sees in Abraham and Abimelech important parallels. She argues that neither cares for the public innocence, but rather each in narrow ways seeks to establish his personal innocence and proclaim guilt on others. "Like Abimelek, Abraham refuses to assume responsibility for his actions; he is no longer a shaper of his identity."

27. Koch, *The Growth of the Biblical Tradition*, 120, refers to Gunkel, who suggests that this story is an "ethnological saga." Gunkel's argument is based in large part on the fact that there is a development of Yahweh as a God of many nations.

be ascertained that Abimelech's confession saves him, it is, nevertheless, noteworthy that Abimelech's plea elicits acknowledgment from Yahweh. The use of "integrity of heart" by Abimelech and the repetition of this phrase by Yahweh in the acknowledgment must not go unnoticed. That Yahweh acknowledges Abimelech in this manner places the latter in the company of "insiders" such as Abraham (Gen 17:1) and Job (Job 1:1). Yet, clearly Yahweh's active intentional involvement saves Sarah, grants Abimelech a chance to live, and acts through the prayer of Abraham in granting fertility to the women of Gerar (v. 17). Before God makes the announcement, the confession of Abimelech is important and God's absolution is a necessary follow-up. One of the narrator's intents is to demonstrate the reciprocal nature of hospitality. One might conclude based on the response of Yahweh, that Abimelech's actions are seen as hospitable. In like manner, Yahweh acts hospitably with Abimelech and the people of Gerar. As serious as is the taking of Sarah by Abimelech, even more serious is the possibility of death that the people of Gerar face. The respective acts of hospitality reflect the magnitude of seriousness. Because of the initial pronouncement of death (v. 3) and the fact that Yahweh is the one who is the architect of Abimelech's hospitable action, it is an extraordinary act by Yahweh allowing Abimelech to live. In the face of death, God chooses life; it is always God's intent that people live (Gen 2:17 and 3:21; Jon 3:4 and 3:11) Even when death is pronounced, the reality is that often the heart of God is changed when approached with repentance and confession and the chance to provide life (cf. 2 Kings 20).

Yahweh's pre-emptive act of grace has a three fold implication in the narrative. First, it saves Sarah from becoming a part of Abimelech's personal harem, and the object of sexual conquest.[28] Second, outside of Abimelech's plea of innocence, it is Yahweh's act of grace that allows him to have new life. The hospitality of Abimelech to Sarah is borne out of Yahweh's actions. Third, the gracious act of God ensures that the ancestress of the promise was not taken away. Moreover, the promise was kept alive, despite Abraham's actions. Abimelech is informed that it was Yahweh who knew his heart; it was Yahweh who kept him from sinning; it was Yahweh who kept him from touching Sarah. The hospitable and gracious party *par excellence* in this narrative is Yahweh.

28. Trible, *God and the Rhetoric of Sexuality*, 34, says, "God acts to save Sarah from male abuse by informing and threatening the king."

Despite the profession of innocence by Abimelech, as recognized and orchestrated by Yahweh, Abimelech will still have to act hospitably in the restoration of Sarah. Indeed the restoration of Sarah is the passport to new life. The fact that in v. 17 Abimelech is told that restoration will ensure continued life for all in Gerar, again, in more explicit fashion his actions are seen to have public consequences.

Throughout the Yahweh-Abimelech dialogue, there is no discussion of Abraham's role and his actions that led to the entire scenario; yet it is Abraham who is given the opportunity to pray for Abimelech and restore the potential for life and continued generations. This is the second example of inversion in the narrative. What is clear here is the reality that Abraham *will* be the promise bearer, not because of his righteousness, or his ideal actions, but rather in spite of them. Abimelech's encounter with Yahweh brings life, but it also makes clear that Yahweh will continue to use Abraham as the one who has been set apart. The issue here is not one of fairness or justice, but rather an expression of God's grace that surpasses human error and distrust.

What is the nature of Yahweh when the one who distrusts and acts without vision is completely exonerated and in fact is not reprimanded, cautioned, corrected or punished?[29] Further, not only does God "intervene so eagerly and decisively,"[30] but Abraham is given a new privilege and responsibility as prophet and mediator. What Yahweh demonstrates to Abimelech and even more extraordinarily to Abraham, is that the divine vision supersedes any such human undertaking, and in the face of hostility, God unequivocally chooses hospitality.

Who Is Afraid of Whom?

The corporate personality of Abimelech, as he attends to the subject of the dream becomes evident. His actions and experience will not only affect him in isolation, but as is the case with leaders, their actions affect their people. The response of the servants, like that of Abimelech, is one of fear that is borne out of the recognition of Yahweh's power. Given the fact that neither the servants nor Abimelech had witnessed

---

29. See White, *Narrative and Discourse*, 184, who notes, however, "The usual juxtaposition of honorable hero versus dishonorable opponent is blurred by the hero's morally questionable strategy."

30. Ibid., 175.

any concrete expressions of death, this recognition of Yahweh is even more stunning. At this point, the narrative indicates that only the men of the household are aware of the dream of Abimelech (v. 8b), and even though later (v. 18), we are told that it was the women who were affected by the actions of Abraham and Sarah, and Abimelech, the news is not told specifically to them. Abimelech's meeting with Abraham positions the latter on the defensive, inducing him to defend his action against Abimelech and the people of Gerar. In his brief engagement with Abraham, Abimelech does not seek to exonerate himself, as he pleads his case (v. 9), but nevertheless pushes Abraham to admit responsibility for the entire sordid episode. But perhaps even more than admission, Abraham is forced to recognize his role in the lives of all the people he has encountered and will encounter on the journey. Abraham who is entrusted to be a blessing to others, also holds the potentiality to bring death. He has to this point demonstrated that he is less likely to trust in the promise and the leading of Yahweh than in his own ingenuity and fear. The result has been disastrous. His fear of Gerar and the established belief that the fear of the Lord is absent in the nation leads him to act in the manner he did. The irony here is that despite Abraham's overarching concern, Abimelech and the people of Gerar do fear Yahweh (vv. 4, 8), and finally it is Abraham's myopia that is being called into question. In comparing the "thrice told tale" in Genesis with 2 Samuel 11, Miscall notes certain parallels and points of continuity. Even though the foreigner is perceived by Abraham as one who might kill him and take his wife, one who does not fear Yahweh, it is Abimelech who voices the moral code. Contrast such acuity with David, the insider, who took another man's wife, made her pregnant, and then committed murder to cover his tracks. David knew the consequences of his actions, yet he proceeded, thinking, with a lack of commitment to the covenant similar to Abraham, only of himself and securing the present. "In 2 Samuel 11, David like the patriarchs, can be accused of immorality, a self-centered narrowness with concern just for the moment."[31]

Despite the lame excuse of Sarah indeed being his sister, his action like the sped arrow, is irreversible. The reality is that Abraham did set out to deceive Abimelech and the people of Gerar in order to save himself. While Abraham's premeditated actions provide the possibility for Sarah's demise (v. 13), they are sharply paralleled by Yahweh's proac-

---

31. Miscall, "Literary Unity in Old Testament Narratives," 39–40.

tive presence on behalf of the promise. While Abraham is the certified promise bearer, and clearly the one who has been given the responsibility to bring blessing and life, it is Abimelech who has imperial power.

Abimelech is aware that Abraham as the one who has been granted the power to restore life to him and his people, chooses to focus on his responsibility in the direct questioning of Abraham. In this context according to Koch, "The king's language is very distinctive when he calls a subordinate to account... The apologetic answer given by a subordinate begins with 'Because I thought' in xx.ii, xxvi.9."[32] It is not surprising that the two main discourses in the narrative take place between those with royal power, Yahweh and Abimelech. In one respect, Abimelech's words to Abraham are meant to be understood not in a narrow provincial way, but in a broader context to enlighten Abraham in the manner in which he approaches others. Even though the first two questions of Abimelech to Abraham are rhetorical, they nevertheless force Abraham to recognize his guilt in this matter. The questions are sharp and to the point. If there is a point of redemption for Abraham, it is his silence in the face of Abimelech's questions. The rhetorical questions, ethical in essence, are heard in silence. Perhaps, this is Abraham's inner and outward acknowledgment of his distrust and fear. Undoubtedly Abimelech is aware that future life depends on Abraham, yet the responsibility to pursue truth cannot be subsumed under personal fear. If Abimelech does not challenge Abraham, then he would indeed be remiss in discharging his responsibility thus replicating the actions of Abraham in a different guise. The fact that Abraham does not contest the questions of Abimelech, together with his answer in vv. 10, 11 testifies to his admission of guilt. The interest of Abimelech at this point is not to enter with Abraham into the type of discourse he had with Yahweh in the dream.[33]

One does not wish to create a hero out of Abimelech; but the text reminds us again and again that the particularity of this encounter has public implications. Abraham's response to Abimelech is not only defensive, but highlights a third example of inversion in the text. Abraham says, "I did it because I thought, there is no fear of God at all in this

---

32. Koch, *The Growth of the Biblical Tradition*, 121.

33. See Westermann, *Genesis 12–36*, 325, who remarks: "Abraham's guilt is neither diminished nor glossed over; the accusations set it in sharp relief. What happens in vv. 14–18 by way of making amends in no wise alters this."

place, and they will kill me because of my wife" (v. 11).³⁴ The irony here is that while Abraham's premeditative action assumes evil on the part of a divergent group, and acts in a manner contrary to the trust he is called to exemplify, it is Abimelech who expresses a "Fear of the Lord." One might say that it is the surprising blindness of the one who is supposed to have "sight" and perceive "truth" in the face of the "outsider" who perceives more accurately (cf. Luke 6:41ff.). "Perception . . . is the crucial issue for Abraham . . . Abraham must define his own destiny, and what he sees must not be guided by his own lack of perception or by the misperception of others."³⁵

Sarah's Ḥesed and the Fear of Yahweh

Many studies have been done on the "Fear of the Lord," the results of which will not be duplicated here.³⁶ One particular element of the "Fear of the Lord" in the present narrative, however, warrants our attention. Abraham's words point directly to the matter of hospitality as the reason for his conclusion.

Abraham's approach to the promise is one in which he views himself as the main, perhaps essential bearer. It is this often unstated belief that prompts him to relegate Sarah to a secondary role and indeed a role that endangers her. Abraham's explanation to Abimelech of his words to Sarah prior to their entrance into Gerar, serves only to undermine the secondary role attributed to Sarah (v. 11). The irony in Abraham's words to Sarah is that he calls upon her *ḥesed* to protect him. His recognition of *ḥesed* in Sarah demonstrates a twofold value.

First, it is the character and partnership of Sarah over the years that lead Abraham to this confident assessment. There is no deliberation here on the part of Abraham wondering about the *ḥesed* of Sarah.

---

34. Marmesh, "Anti-Covenant," 50, observes that, "There is a strange logic in this fabula. The Canaanites are depicted as evil (not God fearing). Yet, they are aware of the taboo against sleeping with someone else's wife. Perhaps this is why they were thought to kill husbands; if the husband is dead, no one has legal rights to the woman and they are free to own her . . . There is duplicity in this taboo. When wife-abduction benefits the patriarchs, it is allowed. If wife-abduction threatens the well-being of the male household, it is disallowed . . . The logic of this fabula is twisted in a way that absolves the males from being condemned or condemning themselves for the trading of women for favors."

35. Steinmetz, *From Father to Son*, 64.

36. See, e.g., Wolff, "Elohistic Fragments," 161–63.

Yet, his narrow sense of others' goodness and hospitality prompts him to call upon a noble characteristic and utilize it for ignoble reasons.

Second, and more directly related to the journey, is a call to have Sarah be faithful not to herself, but to Abraham. "This is the kindness (*ḥesed*) you must do me" (v. 13, NRSV).[37] The NRSV translates *ḥesed* in v. 13 as "kindness," but this choice does not capture the fundamental essence of the word's usage in this particular context. What Abraham seeks is loyalty to himself and not a petitioning of Sarah's integrity. In being loyal to Abraham, according to his standards of loyalty, Sarah will necessarily compromise her own honesty and integrity. Sakenfeld notes: "Although from a sociocultural perspective Sarah was subordinate to her husband (brother), in this particular setting his life was in her hands. Because of their relationship, she had a commitment to him, yet she was free to decide whether or not to perform the act of loyalty requested . . . Loyalty meant being less than completely truthful, for the sake of the other. Abraham asks this of her without any special pleading. It is as if the relationship provides whatever basis is necessary for the request."[38]

In all of this Sarah does not argue. Perhaps she might have, except for the sake of the promise. Sarah is perfectly capable of expressing herself in matters concerning her life, as is witnessed in her reaction to the announcement in 18:12 and her proactive stance in 16:3.[39] In an explicitly extraordinary way, sacrifices are demanded of Sarah for the sake of the promise, while Abraham receives credit as the bearer of the promise. While the sociocultural norms prescribe the role for Sarah, the theological crux of the text calls for our attention. The one who is being sacrificed again and again (v.13 "at every place") functions as servant and in this text itself remains anonymous, and silent (cf. Isa 53:7).

---

37. The NEB renders the statement in v. 13 as, "There is a duty towards me which you must loyally fulfill." The NAB says of the same verse, "Would you do me this favor?"; the NJB translates it, "There is an act of love you can do me"; and the NIV, "This is how you can show your love for me." While all these translations depart from following the Hebrew text closely, the interpretation produced in these instances capture accurately the essence of Abraham's words. The NJB's version in particular calls to mind the contemporary vernacular, "If you truly love me, you will . . . " The overtone of selfishness is self-evident.

38. Sakenfeld, *Faithfulness in Action*, 27.

39. To be sure, in 16:3 she is in the role of one who has power over another, and exercises this power in a proactive manner.

Outside of the narrator's reference to "Sarah," all other references to Sarah throughout the text are done through pronouns. Of particular importance is Abraham's discussion of Sarah in vv. 11–13. While Abraham calls on Sarah to function on the basis of her ḥesed, his own ḥesed appears to be absent in the manner in which he relates with others (vv. 21–23). Sarah's identity is shaped by reference to the men in her life. She is "my wife" (2x); "my sister;" "the daughter of my father." While Abraham undermines the personhood and role of Sarah in the promise, it is Abimelech who demonstrates respect for her. The narrator in pointing to the restoration by Abimelech, notes that it is "Sarah the wife" who is restored. For the promise to continue, it is "Sarah the wife," not "Sarah the sister" who must be restored. On the other hand, Sarah's integrity and loyalty are maintained when Abimelech addresses her. "Look, I have given *your brother* . . ." (v. 16).[40] Thus while Abraham is reminded of his sin and the absolute necessity of Sarah being "wife" rather than "sister," Sarah is indirectly called Abraham's sister by Abimelech and she is the one exonerated. Further, note the extent to which the narrator goes, in order to cast an unblemished Sarah into the future (v. 16b). While the Hebrew expression here is unclear, the intended meaning is certainly clear. The use of the phrase, "to cover the eyes" in reference to Sarah is designed to express fundamentally a justification of Sarah in the eyes of all who might encounter her in the future. Von Rad captures the essence of the Hebrew phraseology when he says, "The gift means that the critical eyes of others will be covered so that they will be unable to discover anything shocking in Sarah."[41]

Abraham is the one to whom the three fold components for shaping one's identity has been given—land, descendants, God (17:8). All three of these elements are in danger as Abraham sacrifices Sarah, alienates himself with Abimelech, distrusts God's leading and, without the hospitality of Abimelech, has no land in which to live. This is the fourth example of inversion in the narrative. Abimelech, the outsider, not only fears God but further, maintains the proper relationship between Abraham and Sarah. Through his restoration (and because of divine intervention), he provides a land for the foreigners. It is the outsider who

---

40. Niditch, *Underdogs and Tricksters*, 57, views this reference in quite an opposite fashion when she says, "The king refers to the hero as the woman's brother in verse 16, an implicit reminder that the hero never lied." I find Niditch's conclusion at this point less than persuasive.

41. Von Rad, *Genesis*, 229.

comes to understand the elements that shape identity. As if to underline this inversion, Abimelech goes beyond the restoration of Sarah, to the freedom of choice for a place to live within the land.[42] Abimelech's actions, both by way of the grand gifts and the invitation to live within the land can only be classified as extravagant hospitality.[43] This act of giving land to Abraham further underlines the irony in the narrative, for Abraham who once feared for his life in coming into Gerar, now ceases to be a routine visitor, and settles in the land to reside for a while. In order for life to continue in Gerar, the only necessary item on Yahweh's agenda was the restoration of Sarah. Given the fact that Yahweh extends to Abimelech the extravagant hospitality of life, it is likely that this is the influence that prompts Abimelech to do likewise.[44]

From Curse to Blessing

The final section of the narrative (vv. 16–18) brings into sharp focus the precise importance of Sarah. While Sarah has been portrayed as an accessory in the plot against Abimelech, her role has been designed by Abraham. However, as the narrative comes to a close it becomes apparent that it is the crime against Sarah for which the people of Gerar are punished.[45] Even though Abimelech is told by Yahweh that restoration will save him from death, it is not until v. 17 that "life" is spelled out. That "life," as promised to Abimelech was not only the continuation of the present existence of the people of Gerar, but the future of Gerar itself. Note the unmistakable co-relation between the danger of the

42. Unlike Gen 12:19–20, where Abraham is asked to leave Egypt.

43. Contra Niditch, *Underdogs and Tricksters*, 56, who argues, "On the typological level one sees that the author of Genesis 20 seeks to portray the heroes as 'high class' . . . as royalty, equal to their counterpart in Gerar and deserving of the latter's large financial settlement for their trouble."

44. Sternberg, *The Poetics of Biblical Narrative*, 316, deduces that, "The surprise ending drives home to the reader that Abimelech is after all just another Pharaoh, likewise prevented from violating Sarah only by great plagues inflicted on him by God." That there is divine intervention in both accounts is not in question, though the parallels between Pharaoh and Abimelech are not nearly as prominent as Sternberg intimates.

45. See Polzin, "'The Ancestress of Israel in Danger,'" 86: "What is interesting here in the Gen 20 version is that there is an explicit connection made between the adulterous situation and infertility: God had closed all their wombs of the house of Abimelech because of the apparent adultery. Once that situation was removed, Abimelech's household immediately become fertile (20:17) and Sarah herself, for a long time infertile, now becomes pregnant."

ancestress of Israel and the future of the promise, and the closing of the wombs of all the women. The connection between the two is further punctuated by the fact that neither the women of Gerar nor Sarah is made barren because of their sin, but rather through circumstances beyond their control. Trible observes that, "with the liberation of Sarah, divine blessing comes to the other females. Yahweh who has closed wombs in judgment for sin opens them for fertility."[46] Further, it is to be noted that even though sheep, oxen, slaves and Sarah herself are given to Abraham, the major issue at stake only comes in v. 16.[47]

The fact that Sarah is given to Abraham along with other "property" reminds us of the nature of the society. In v.16, however, the narrator ensures that the reader recognizes that for a satisfactory closure to the entire matter the complete exoneration of Sarah, and the establishing of her innocence are required. While "patriarchal ownership" in v. 15 is a sociocultural phenomenon, the theological issue that is to bring life is set apart in v. 16. Not surprising therefore, it is only after Sarah's name is cleared that Abraham prays to God. Here too, the emphasis is not on Abraham, but on the role and presence of God. One notes that in the entire narrative, Abraham is not told that he is to pray for the wellbeing of the people of Gerar. That was only made known to Abimelech and he does not say a word about it to Abraham. It is God who brings about the healing. Indeed, the narrative never says that Abraham is repentant or for that matter that he changes his attitude towards foreigners. Finally however, that is not the issue in the story. God will in fact continue to use Abraham despite his actions. The final issue at stake is the recognition of Sarah's innocence. Abimelech's direct address to her, referring to Abraham as "her brother" maintains Abraham's guilt, but erases Sarah's complicity. By referring to Abraham as "her brother," Abimelech indicates that he understands the predicament in which she was placed.

---

46. Trible, *God and the Rhetoric of Sexuality*, 34, is surely correct in terms of the biblical picture of "sin" leading to infertility; but there is no such evidence in the particular case of these women.

47. See Peterson, "A Thrice-Told Tale," 40, who concludes that, "Even with the payment and promise of land rights, the issue of who is right and who is wrong, who was the ultimate perpetrator of sin, is left sardonically ambiguous . . . No one could be singled out as guilty, and yet it is quite clear that Elohim has been seriously affronted. This is the dialectic of sin."

5

Silence of the Lamb

Genesis 22

I FIRST ENCOUNTERED THE POEM *CASABIANCA* BY FELICIA DOROTHEA Hemans (1793–1835) as a nine-year-old boy and memorized it as a class requirement. It was the text and theme of this poem that have been deeply and perhaps permanently etched on my mind. The following excerpt sets the scene of indescribable horror.

> The boy stood on the burning deck,
> Whence all but him had fled;
> The flame that lit the battle's wreck,
> Shone round him o'er the dead.
>
> The flames roll'd on—he would not go
> Without his father's word;
>
> He call'd aloud—"say father, say
> If yet my task be done!"
>
> "Speak father!" once again he cried,
> "If I may yet be gone!"
>
> And shouted but once more aloud,
> "My father! must I stay?"
>
> There came a burst of thunder sound—
> The boy—oh! Where was he?
> Ask of the winds that far around
> With fragments strewed the sea.

With mask, and helm and pennon fair,
That well had borne their part;
But the noblest thing that perished there
Was that young faithful heart.
(excerpts from stanzas 1, 3–6, 9–10)

As this poem was taught to us, the primary interest was in conveying the theme of unflinching obedience. It was a lesson in moral rectitude. For this nine year old, the horror of such a holocaust under the guise of obedience has never left my memory bank. It is a narrative of horror. As I read Genesis 22, the parallels are striking, if only in an extrinsic manner.

Genesis 22 has traditionally been cited as one of the extraordinary moments in the Abraham narrative. Indeed the very nature of this text has made it painful to explore. Among the multitude of problematic hermeneutical matters that the Hebrew Bible posits before us, the "testing" of Abraham i.e., the potential sacrifice of Isaac is one of the most difficult. The idea of child sacrifice to please God seems contrary to tradition-shaped notions of who God is, and simultaneously contrary to what it means to be bonded in human fidelity. When confronted by a God who would be well pleased with, and well served by child sacrifice, both of the above mentioned perceptions lose all integrity. In its horrific implications, we are challenged to re-think yet again the theological undergirding and meaning of the *imago dei*.[1]

Historically, the traditional focus of this text within Christianity has been on the unflappable faith of Abraham; the obedience of Abraham in the face of a monstrous test. In the Jewish tradition, the interpretive interest has surrounded the binding of Isaac, the *Akedah*. There has been precious little in any sustained way that has challenged these particular foci. Indeed within the context of religious education over the centuries the concept of faith is so well entrenched that we have been blinded to other critical possibilities within this text.[2]

---

1. Johnson, *She Who Is*, 4, suggests: "God is that on which you lean your heart, that on which your heart depends, 'that to which your heart clings and entrusts itself,' in Martin Luther's memorable phrase."

2. See Brueggemann, "Preaching to Exiles," 5. Speaking to the role of the church and its resistance to radical but necessary change, and its appropriation of painful and sometimes forgotten biblical metaphors, Brueggemann advances a proposition which not only has implications for the church, but for the scholarly world as well. He suggests

However in recent times, both Jewish and Christian scholarship has raised critical questions, at once uneasy and painful, but at the same time absolutely persistent and timely if indeed we are to take this text seriously and unearth the breadth of theological possibilities. Crenshaw perceptively identifies an important dichotomy in the manner in which God is seen by both Christian and Jewish traditions. While the God of the Hebrew Bible is seen as a compassionate God, one of the often-overlooked biblical components is the numerous references that portray God as wrathful and violent. The issue here is not whether God is compassionate or whether God changes his mind to give life. In fact there is an abundance of instances that testify to this (e.g., Exod 34:6–7a; Jer 32:18; Jon 4:2b). But the question relates to the manner in which we reconcile the compassion of God and the violence of God.[3] God in the Hebrew Bible is pictured as one who is to be trusted. This idea further compounds the horrific nature of the test for the origin of the horror is from God, the very one who asks for trust, who is to be trusted. This is the type of ambiguity and one-sided direction that leads Crenshaw to question whether God might be fickle. Indeed he refers to Genesis 22 as a "monstrous test."[4]

Recently, Trible has raised the issue of Sarah's sacrifice as a central theme in this text. Trible argues that, "If Laughter (Isaac) is special to Abraham, how much more to Sarah! She claims the child for herself, 'for me.' After all he is hers, not Abraham's one and only son . . . Unlike the bond between Sarah and Isaac, no unique tie exists here between Abraham and Isaac."[5] Trible argues that the attachment between Abraham and Isaac enters into the realm of idolatry. It is unnatural and indeed if there were to be any natural attachment to Isaac it should

---

that the challenge which faces us is to counter the 'culture of denial' which continues to imagine that it is as it was, even when our experience tells us otherwise." In something of a different view, see Breech, *The Silence of Jesus*, 11, who in pursuit of the historical Jesus asks, "How do we get to where we are not from where we are? The journey if it is to be one of discovery will entail a certain amount of dispossession, that is of a readiness to re-examine and perhaps to abandon the assumptions which inform our customary modes of questioning."

3. See Crenshaw, *A Whirlpool of Torment*.

4. Ibid., 9. See also, Humphreys, *The Tragic Vision and the Hebrew Tradition*, 81, who suggests that this kind of testing portrays a God who takes "no apparent account of human parental feelings."

5. Trible, "Genesis 22," 186–87.

be with Sarah.⁶ Overarching evidence abounds in the Genesis narratives that, in fact, Abraham is *not* a man of strong attachments. That Abraham was willing to leave without question (Gen 12:4) might be an expression of great faith or one lacking in strong attachment.⁷ While the former has dominated the scholarly and lay avenues of interpretation, the latter has only recently gained deserved attention. The issue here is not whether Abraham had faith or whether he was a person with little or no concern for attachment to family or place.⁸ Indeed as we think of this issue regardless of gender, we would be well served to reflect on the journey of many of our ancestors who came to the United States not so much out of extraordinary necessity or lack of care for the land of birth, but often because of a dream for the future. Often the spirit of a person is so indelibly tied to the land of one's birth that immigration does not change that.

Prior to Trible and Crenshaw, both Jewish and Christian scholars recognized that this text explodes with ethical overtones that transcend faith matters. However, many of their conclusions circumvented the painful directions and settled for the variations of the status quo.

---

6. Ibid., 178–79, advances the thesis that, "Attachment threatened the obedience, the worship, the fear of God. Thus the test offers Abraham an opportunity for healing, an opportunity to free both himself and his son. To attach oneself to another is to negate love through entrapment. In surrounding Isaac, Abraham binds himself and his son. To attach is to know the anxiety of separation. In clinging to Isaac, Abraham incurs the risk of losing him—and Isaac suspects it. To attach is to practice idolatry. In adoring Isaac, Abraham turns from God. The test, then, is an opportunity for understanding and healing. To relinquish attachment is to discover freedom." In something of an interesting twist, Moshe Yeres, "The Meaning of Abraham's Test," 6, posits the argument that, "the test of the Akedah was specifically created by God to bring Abraham closer to his son, to forge a bond of love between Abraham and Isaac."

7. Rosenberg, *King and Kin*, 96, notes that, "Throughout the Abraham cycle, Abraham is shown severing from kin and household in more than one way: leaving his father's house, temporarily losing his kindred wife to a foreign king, expelling Hagar and Ishmael, offering up Isaac, burying Sarah. Erosion of the family seems a constant process and constant threat." While one may find reason to question some of the choices which comprise Rosenberg's list, there is surely evidence that his general thesis is legitimate.

8. See Hampson, "On Power and Gender," 234, quoting Carol Gilligan, *In a Different Voice*, argues that, "Men think in terms of isolated self . . . They are at the centre of their world and they see the world in relation to themselves. What is threatening is that others should come too close." Part of the benefit of a study such as Gilligan's or Hampson's is that it calls and challenges society to look again with new vision on gender roles and characterization. A deeply rooted flaw is the over-generalization.

In particular Kierkegaard's work, *Fear and Trembling* comes to mind. Kierkegaard's notion of the suspension of the ethical in this instance does not get to the issue at hand. No mere philosophical reflection can suffice in the face of such a horrendous request.[9] In somewhat of a similar vein, Kant argues that a moral God would never make such an immoral request. Thus, he concludes God could not possibly make such a request. "There are certain cases in which man is convinced that it cannot be God whose voice he thinks he hears; when the voice commands him to do what is opposed to the moral law though the phenomenon seems to him ever so majestic and surpassing the whole of nature he must count it a deception."[10] Even this philosophical position, while daring in its challenge does not pursue and address the issue of power and marginality.

The daring directions raised by Crenshaw and Trible, along with philosophers such as Kant and Kierkegaard, are to be taken seriously and pursued. The presence of material such as this in the Hebrew Bible invites—perhaps even impels us—to engage the message with all of its complexity, tensions and ambiguity and enter into the lives of these people. Not to do so is to insult both the memory and experiences of these our ancestors.[11]

In this study, the intent is to demonstrate the separation and rings of power that exist between those who function at the center and those who live at the margin. In this way, the issue is not focused solely on the conspicuous and inexplicable absence of Sarah (itself a problematic matter) or on God's testing (a painful centrality in the story), but rather the larger issue of the structure and execution of the power—powerless dichotomy, and the cast of players who constitute each camp. There are fairly well delineated levels of power, and one notices this particularly with Abraham, for while he clearly has power, he is also one called upon to obey commands. Sarah is invisible and voiceless and while Isaac is allowed the freedom to ask questions, he exists as an object and is not

---

9. See Søren Kierkegaard, *Fear and Trembling*.

10. As quoted by Westermann, *Genesis 12–36*, 354.

11. See Plank, "The Survivor's Return," 269. Reflecting on the erasing of the holocaust memory, Plank's insights also bear critical witness to the importance of taking seriously the stories of our ancestors. Their stories cannot be overlooked or misconstrued for propriety purposes. Plank suggests, "Those who facilely beautify, clean and construct on profane ground risk becoming like those who, in 1943, planted pines at Sobibor: agents of illusion who oppose the truth of remembrance and return."

privy to the plans for the sacrifice.[12] Both Sarah and Isaac are kept in the dark with decisions being made on their behalf without an invitation to speak. Voicelessness as a reflection of powerlessness is deafening in this text.

A Unique Test?

These seemingly routine opening verses to a narrative are filled with terrifying ambiguity and fear. Even to a casual reader the horror of what is to transpire must leap out. In any discussion of this text, one may not reduce the test to Abraham's unquestioning response.[13]

"After these things, God tested . . ." (v. 1). As this text begins, one senses that the narrator is implying that this is the first time that Abraham is being tested. The pronouncement of such a "test" ought to take the reader by surprise. After all Abraham and Sarah had been severely tested before.[14] Thus, if there is to be a surprise it should be because "testing" has already been executed in extreme and fearful ways, or so we are led to believe. One must wonder what is at stake in this "test" for God. We know that God's intent is not to ill Isaac, but to test Abraham. Given this we are led to believe that this something if a risk for God and for the sake of unquestionable trust, God become vulnerable.

It appears that all of the experiences that shaped the journey of Abraham and Sarah to this point are reduced to one nondescript phrase, "After these things"! While this phrase is used elsewhere in the Hebrew Bible (e.g., Gen 15:1; 39:7), in this text the very routine, casual three-word encapsulation of a painful journey stands as a sharp counterpoint to the horrific test that is to transpire. For the first time, and indeed the only time, does the Hebrew *nissah* ("test") appear.[15] Both literarily and

---

12. Kierkegaard, *Fear and Trembling*, 185, suggests that Abraham in response to Isaac's questions essentially says nothing. "His reply to Isaac has the form of irony, for it always is irony when I say something and do not say anything."

13. For a brief history of exegesis of this text, see Westermann, *Genesis 12–36*, 353–54.

14. Trible, "Genesis 22," 171, catalogs the torments of Abraham and Sarah thus: "Barrenness, deception, warfare, surrogacy, manipulation, destruction, incest, jealousy, envy, rivalry, and malice . . ."

15. With the exception of two instances (Ps 26:2; 2 Chron 32:31) both considered late, all uses of *nissah* in the Hebrew Bible have Israel as object of Yahweh's testing.

theologically, *nissah* in Gen 22:1 abruptly ushers in a hitherto untold notion. This will not be a test of conventional proportions, and given the experiences which Abraham and Sarah had previously endured, the magnitude and variety of which would last for generations, we are left wondering: what could possibly transpire now. Trible concludes, "It portends a crisis beyond usual tumult."[16] Given the nature of the usage of *nissah* in the Hebrew Bible, where the emphasis is on the relationship between Yahweh and Israel—that is, focusing on the issue of community, and the people as a collective entity—we are led to believe that this critical test will shift the focus from individual attachment to corporate responsibility. Thus another complicating component of the narrative enters, further compounding the complexity. Abraham must not only face the reality of a father/son relationship being placed under extraordinary strain, but also be reminded that he is the father of "multitudes." Will Abraham be able to endure the test? This question captures the overt scenario. In this obvious and traditionally well-established scenario, the one who stands to gain or lose is Abraham. However, we are aware from both the previous experiences and the nature of the society, that Abraham has a degree of power; by virtue of having a voice, he has, to some extent a measure of control.[17]

Thus, as we shall see, *nissah* involves more than Abraham. The degree and nature of the tests vary tremendously for Isaac and Sarah, as both are powerless and voiceless. Sarah is invisible and Isaac has not been invited into either the planning scheme or the conversation. Abraham never addresses Isaac. Isaac is the initiator of any and all conversation. While this test may appear to be legitimate as far as the faith of Abraham is concerned, it certainly gives rise to the question of the ethical nature of God's testing that is predicated on the abuse of Isaac and Sarah.

16. Trible, "Genesis 22," 171.

17. See Kohn, "The Trauma of Isaac," 96, who notes, "Abraham as the text portrays him is always in a *hineni* state of readiness to do God's bidding: ready to transgress the limits of human compassion for the sake of obedience *ad absurdam*. This 'leap of faith' which is the result of suspension of the ethical, as Kierkegaard would argue, has been unsettling. It seems that all the arguments in the Midrash fall short in reconciling our conception of a just and compassionate God, with God's demand to Abraham that he commit such a monstrous act." Looking at the test with a different interpretive eye, Soelle, *Suffering*, 30, suggests that, "The writer is trying to overcome the archaic picture of God as one who is pleased with human sacrifices. God is not one who commands the absurd, even though that appears to be the case. People are not compelled to suspend the ethical." At one level one feels inclined to agree with Soelle, and yet the canonical text defies such a comfortable assessment.

Silence of the Lamb 109

The excruciating degree of the test is immediately pronounced in the context of the father/son relationship. Even in v. 1 we are alerted that Isaac's life is potentially tested away between two sources of power. Yahweh is the one with ultimate power and throughout the Abraham narrative, it is Yahweh who promises particulars, is faithful in fulfillment and determines directions. However throughout the Abraham narrative we see strong evidence of Abraham's challenge to this power (e.g., Genesis 18) and thus a very particular precedent for responding to Yahweh's request is established. Yet, Abraham's only response is *hinneni* ("Here I am")! Is not this the same Abraham who passionately and with great risk challenged Yahweh on behalf of Sodom? Did God not listen? Was the mind of God not changed? Even in the context of a powerplay, one with some degree of power through a voice spoke on behalf of the voiceless! Yet, Abraham, again with a degree of power, does not challenge or question; he simply responds with *hinneni*! This time, in sharp contradistinction, he uses his voice for compliance.

Further, one is impelled to enquire about the absence of Sarah. At such a critical moment in this narrative Sarah is absent. She is not even behind the door listening! The lines are drawn immediately in v. 1. While Isaac is the object of the "test", this challenge involves Yahweh and Abraham. Isaac is described as Abraham's only son, the one whom he loves. Even here under the guise of a father-son relationship the politics of exclusion are operative. We already know that in fact Isaac is *not* the only son, for there is also Ishmael, and moreover the phrase "whom you love," designed to pronounce the level of pain which this test will bring about, injects a further divisive component. The Hebrew *yachîd* rendered "only" in this text clearly cannot be taken literally. Rather *yachîd* in this instance must be rendered "unique" or *sui generis*, in the sense that he is *the* one to carry the promise. There is something remarkably subtly coercive about this statement. God speaks on behalf of Abraham, determining for him his love of son. Yet, Abraham is perfectly capable of determining his love and speaking on his own behalf. In casting a singular prominence on Isaac, Ishmael's memory is eroded. Those with power have the capacity to remember or to banish from memory; in memory and inclusion there is life.[18] Once before, Ishmael along with

---

18. Bal, *Death and Dissymmetry*, 60, notes that, "Modern logic is called to obscure an ideologically disturbing message. It is Yahweh, who, in Gen. 22:2, uses the word; in the eyes of the twentieth century scholar, the bypassing of the older child is unfair;

Hagar was sacrificed and we know that Abraham was distressed (Gen 21:11). In the face of what appears to be a brutal sacrifice, silence reigns! But this silence is fused to an ongoing voiceless role of Isaac.

Indeed, a critical component of the drama and poignancy that envelop this narrative involves the innocence of Isaac. This "Laughter" in the lives of Abraham and Sarah will in fact also embody extraordinary grief and tragedy. We are already aware that this "Laughter" unknowingly was the center of the furor that led to Hagar and Ishmael's exile. Again, in Genesis 22, Isaac remains essentially unenlightened, his very life in jeopardy, at once unknowingly the cause, at once unknowingly the object of banishment.

The language of v. 2 reminds us that God is aware of the extraordinary nature of the test. The command "to take" is tempered with the use of *na'*. Through the use of *na'*, there is a sense that God implores Abraham to undertake the test. If the horrific nature of the test leads God to implore, how much more difficult must it have been for Abraham! In the face of divine imploring, is the human being able to refuse? Precisely in this context of a monstrous test we detect the faint echo of acknowledgment that God understood the magnitude of the request.[19] In these verses the intent of the narrator is not to spell out the details of the actual sacrifice; nor to embellish the narrative with excessive discourse between God and Abraham or Abraham and Isaac. Statements are made; questions are implied and the reader is left to draw conclusions. In significant ways there is a profound invitation to question.[20] In the raising of theological and sociological questions the textual waters may be muddied, but there would be integrity in reading the text.

Distancing and Deception

Abraham's response is reminiscent of Gen 21:14 where he rises early to send into exile both Hagar and Ishmael. It was an act of death. There

---

hence he is not willing to ascribe it to deity . . . Isaac is called the only child with a clear purpose: to convey that Ishmael does not count."

19. Crenshaw, *A Whirlpool of Torment*, 14. Also Sarna suggests that *na'* "usually softens the command to an entreaty . . . Abraham has absolute freedom of choice. Should he refuse, he would not incur any guilt," *Genesis*, 151. One must wonder whether Abraham did in fact have a choice.

20. See Collins, "Naming God in Public Prayer," 291, who notes: "One of the best gifts for the critical mind and for a living tradition is the gift of a new question."

is language of urgency here and we are left to wonder whether such language simply demonstrates Abraham's extraordinary obedience or conversely and with deeper complexity we have yet another component of the silence to deceive.[21] Could it be that in this way Abraham would not have to face Sarah and tell her of the test on which he was embarking? There is no reason to conclude on the basis of the narrative that Abraham was moved by religiosity or the urgency of the need for the sacrifice of his son.[22]

As we begin v. 3 there is a systematic development of the theme of distancing. While clearly "rising early" denotes attentiveness to God's command, I would like to advance the thesis that, as part of the drama and horror of the event, distancing takes place at different levels. Note four points in this regard.

First, the temporal urgency is countered in the text through the ordering sequence of the constituents necessary for the sacrifice. After saddling the donkey, the primary object of *yiqqah* is "two young men," with "his son Isaac" the last component. The only interest by God in v. 2 is Isaac; God does not outline the necessary elements. Yet, in v. 3 there is a sense of formality and order. Already, there is distancing that takes place between Abraham (one with power) and Isaac (powerless).

Second, as Abraham and the entourage leave for the unknown destination in the distance, the sense of separation and distancing leaps out. Thus, in v. 3 the place is "in the distance" and in v. 4 Abraham saw the place "far away." The further Abraham moves *towards* his destination, the greater the distance *from* Sarah. While the "third day" inference here alludes to the wider biblical usage of this notion, pointing to the sealing of relationships and the granting of new life,[23] there is the

---

21. See Bodoff, "The Real Test of the *Akedah*." Bodoff argues that in fact Abraham was so reluctant to carry out this test that he stalled. "The text can be interpreted to show Abraham stalling. It does not show Abraham leaping from receipt of God's command to his execution of it," ibid., 78.

22. See Brisman, who observes that it is possible to "fill in several motives for this attentiveness to the divine injunction. Either Abraham is solicitous about Hagar and eager to see her settled somewhere before sundown, or he is interested in getting the whole nasty business of his hands, or he hastens to obey a divine command. In turning to the Isaac story, we seem to be viewing a purified zeal, for since there is no quest of kindly regard for the future of *this* outcast, pious attentiveness seems to be the reason for Abraham's haste," *The Voice of Jacob*, 57.

23. See, e.g., Exod 3:18; Jonah 1:17 and the multitude of New Testament references to the resurrection motif.

odor of death in this text, the death of Sarah and the death of Isaac. Sarah has been exiled in her own house!

Third, the sense of distancing is further amplified in v. 5 even as the rings of power are further delineated. The servants of Abraham (*naʿarîm*) are told to wait. As one would expect, the servants do not have a voice. They are simply told what to do. As was the custom in the Ancient Near Eastern tradition, servants are essentially owned, hence in v. 3 and v. 5 we have *naʿarîm*, his servants. These servants belong to Abraham, and are at the bottom of the power scale; even when they are present, their voices are silent. The characterization of Isaac in v. 5 is remarkably revealing in that Abraham refers to him as *naʿar*. That *naʿar* is used to refer to both the servants and Isaac is singularly significant as the element of anonymity enters in with regard to Isaac. As Isaac becomes anonymous, it is clear that distancing is further established.[24] Moreover, anonymity is a central factor associated with a marginalized existence, for in sacrificing a person, it is certainly easier to do so while creating distancing and anonymity.[25] Under most circumstances anonymity is undesirable, and whether it is assigning of numbers to prisoners or the use of generic term such as "boy," power distinctions are established and maintained. Abraham is one with power and even though Yahweh is the one who brings about the test, the manner in which Abraham addresses those in his midst underlines the levels of power. The silence of the three "young men" in Abraham's company is deafening.

Fourth, maintaining an element of secrecy, Abraham proceeds with the "test." He surprisingly outlines the plan for his servants. As we notice in v. 5 however, there is a note of deception. While both

---

24. Of the eleven references to the person of Isaac in this text, only on two occasions does Abraham speak directly to Isaac, and here the reference is to "my son" (vv. 7, 8). On one other occasion (v. 5) he refers to Isaac as "the boy." There are two noteworthy aspects to these references. First, there is the quality of distancing evidenced here. Even though the relational language of "my son" expresses a degree of kinship, a sense of distancing is clearly in place. Moreover, the instances in vv. 7, 8 are in formalized language. Second, Abraham's language of distance is set in sharp relief against the references to Isaac by God, the angel and the narrator.

25. See Trible who proposes that, "Otherness undercuts oneness; detachment vies with attachment. Establishing distance *naʿar* avoids the pain of paternal bonding," "Genesis 22," 174. Note also Genesis 25 where Abraham is said to have sent away all his sons. While maintaining the focus on Isaac as the promise bearer is laudable, the instances of detachment by Abraham give a particular shape to who he is.

Abraham and Isaac are going to the unspecified destination, we already know the nature of the test. Yet, Abraham tells the servants that the plan is to worship, subsequent to which both he and Isaac will return. On the one hand, one might conclude that Abraham is so confident of the outcome of this test that he assures the servants that both father and son will return. If this were the case then the entire "test" scenario would be a farce with even greater horrific overtones. In this scenario not only are the servants deceived, but also Isaac. The servants are given an itinerary, but not the truth. Isaac who would be the "sacrificial lamb" is deceived by both greater powers. The second scenario poses no fewer hermeneutical problems. Does Abraham intentionally deceive Isaac and the servants? One thinks of the U.S. State Department briefings where often the truth is not divulged for "security reasons." There is a sense that both Yahweh and Abraham engage in a degree of deception to execute the plan without too many raised suspicions.

The narrator does not indicate that Abraham and Isaac discussed the matter of sacrifice, yet it is clear that Isaac is aware of the sacrifice, though not fully. No one but Abraham is fully aware and he goes beyond what Yahweh has told him. It is Abraham's idea to weave a tale of deception.[26] But why? Is Abraham so aware of the horror of this event that there is fear? This deed is such an inordinate experience that the young men must not be aware of it.[27] That there is deception in Genesis 22 and that Abraham in this instance and God in 1 Sam. 16:2 could be involved in deception have prompted both Jewish and Christian traditions to refute vehemently such a theologically problematic notion. Rather, tradition has created and continues to sustain a positive hermeneutic as operative. One may conclude that the gravity of choosing and anointing a new king, even while a king is still legitimately on the throne, parallels the sacrifice of the one who would be the promise bearer. Both of these experiences are profoundly personal, while at the same bearing national and international significance.

Under the guise of providing a land, descendants and blessing, the promise bearer is about to be sacrificed. Can this be a paradigm for seeking to understand why certain expressions of suffering exist? As

---

26. Recall the choosing and anointing of David, a matter so momentous and radical, bordering on anarchy, that Samuel sets out under a cloak of deception (1 Sam 16:2).

27. For a brief discussion of human sacrifice, see Westermann, *Genesis 12–36*, 357–58.

we have seen here and in *Job*, God initiates tests of the faithful. The issue is not to create faithfulness in either Abraham or Job. They are already faithful and thus in both instances it is for God's sake that the test is implemented. Will the human being ever be able to fulfill God's expectations?

The Burden of Death

One of the great ironies in this text is the constraint under which Isaac is placed to carry the essential material for his sacrifice, demonstrating something of a visible union between the two.[28] If, in fact as Trible suggests, Abraham sought to protect Isaac, one is left to wonder how it is that Abraham could lead him to his death. Isaac and Abraham carry all of the elements necessary for the sacrifice. The two principal parties involved in the actual sacrifice are the ones responsible for physically bearing the burden. The sense of distancing continues here as the servants are excluded from any involvement in the sacrifice. Under normal circumstances, the servants would carry any equipment, but this is no ordinary circumstance. Moreover the wood for the sacrifice is the "heavy equipment" necessary for the sacrifice. The young Isaac is made to suffer as a prelude to the sacrifice. One cannot help but see this experience as a precursor to the suffering and crucifixion in the Christian tradition.[29] Jesus Christ is made to carry the cross through the streets, and like Jesus who did not carry the hammer and nails,

---

28. Trible seeks to outline the various levels of danger with regard to the elements necessary for the sacrifice. "Isaac carries the wood that would ignite him. Yet, unkindled it is not dangerous material, unlike the fire and the knife that Abraham takes in his own hands. The father embraces his son with potential destruction even as he protects him from immediate danger." "Genesis 22," 175. That Abraham sought to protect Isaac by carrying the fire and the knife is at best debatable.

29. See Vermes, *Scripture and Tradition in Judaism*. Within the Jewish tradition, Vermes notes, "the binding of Isaac was thought to have played a unique role in the economy of the salvation of Israel, and to have a permanent redemptive effect on behalf of its people. The merits of his sacrifice were experienced by the Chosen People in the past, invoked in the present, and hoped for at the end of time," 208. With regard to the Christian tradition, Vermes indicates that, "The Akedah was considered a sacrifice of redemption, the source of pardon, salvation and eternal life . . . principally through the merits of Isaac, who offered his life voluntarily to his Creator . . . For Paul, the Akedah prophesied a higher truth, a divine mystery revealed in Christ," 220. On the connection between the Atonement and Christ and the sacrifice of Isaac, see Dahl, *Jesus the Christ*, 137–51.

Isaac did not carry the fire and knife. It is the wood, the basis for the sacrifice, which he carried. The wood, like the cross, carries with it a representation and symbol. The heaviness of the burden alludes to the weight of being the object of sacrifice. The irony is further perpetuated as the closeness demonstrated by "walking together" is countered by the distance that continued to be extended. After the stylized formal exchange in v. 7, we are told that they walked on together. They are close together, but worlds apart. To suggest that a bond developed between Abraham and Isaac during this time is to cast an artificial shadow over this text.[30] Regarding v. 6, Wiesel encapsulates the reality thus: "One went to face death, the other to give it, but they went together; still close to one another though everything already separated them."[31] Walking together in silence may connote closeness, but not in this context. In Wiesel's *Night*, he relates poignantly the experience of finding his father in the confines of the concentration camp after he thought they had been separated forever. "He was standing near the wall, bowed down, his shoulders sagging as though beneath a heavy burden. I went to him, took his hand and kissed it. A tear fell upon it. Whose was that tear? Mine? His? I said nothing. Nor did he. We had never understood one another so clearly."[32] Wiesel and his father in the context of a holocaust were silent as they held each other. It was the essence of closeness and a bonding of the spirit. In the face of Isaac's holocaust, there is also silence and togetherness, but finally distance prevails!

Isaac's question as to the whereabouts of the lamb further indicates his knowledge as to what constitutes sacrifice. For the three days of the silent journey, no word is spoken and now that they are alone, Isaac asks what is no more than a practical question. Where is the lamb? Abraham's response is again lacking in specifics. It might be as Brueggemann suggests that Abraham finally does not know and therefore cannot answer absolutely.[33] Absolute certainty with regard to the future is the prerogative of God. Yet, Abraham tells Isaac less than he knows. That Isaac accepts his father's word without question is an astonishing and unwavering expression of faith. At one level, the faith of

---

30. Contra Yeres, who suggests that, "The crisis of the Akedah brings father and son together," "The Meaning of Abraham's Test," 9.

31. Wiesel, "The Sacrifice of Isaac," 81.

32. Wiesel, *Night*, 1960, 79.

33. Brueggemann, *Genesis*, 128.

both father and son in God's provision is resolute. Short of turning back and taking matters into their own hands, Abraham and Isaac have no choice but to believe. The very fine line between knowing all along that God will provide and the uncertainty of such a horrible event is one that Abraham must walk. To tilt in the direction of absolute knowledge of what will transpire is to lie blatantly to Isaac and to make the whole journey a farce. Conversely, to assume that indeed Isaac will be killed is to be engaged in a heinous crime, emotionless. Neither is acceptable, and so, literally and otherwise father and son "walked together" into the unknown.

The levels of power in this story are further underlined through the metaphors of "sight" and "distance." Note two points in this regard. First, in v. 4 after a lapse of three days, Abraham is able to see (*ra'ah*) the appointed place of the sacrifice. Abraham's ability to "see" is limited and in this instance has spatial particularity. Of some import is the narrator's very terse and pointed description in v. 4: it is only Abraham who "sees" the place. This verse speaks of nothing else. With this vision, Abraham asserts his power immediately and directs those with less power. While on this occasion both the servants and Isaac could technically "see" the place in the distance it is not reported thus. In v. 13, the situation is radically transformed, and the suspenseful atmosphere is relieved to a degree, but it is only Abraham who "sees" the ram. Indeed in this setting, physically incapacitated, Isaac is simply unable to see. The narrator creates a systematic outline of the levels of power. As if to underline the secondary tier of Abraham's power, we are reminded that it is God who showed him the site. (v. 9) This follows on the heels of Abraham's response to Isaac's question in v. 8 that God will provide (*ra'ah*).[34]

Second, Abraham assures Isaac that God will provide. This is a confessional statement which transcends faith and establishes power. It was God who provided the place of sacrifice, initially a place which took Abraham three days to see. That God will provide a lamb again points to Yahweh's wide ranging power. Abraham could not "see" the place of the sacrifice and it would not be until the eleventh hour that he would "see" the ram. The choice of "provide" to render *ra'ah* captures the double intent in the use of this term. God not only "sees" but there

---

34. Sarna, translates *'elohim yireh-lô* (v. 8), "God will see." In v. 14a the phrase *adonai yireh* remains untranslated while in v. 14b *yere'eh* is translated "vision" (*Genesis*, 153–54). In all of these renderings the "sight" metaphor is preserved.

is an element of limitless vision associated with God's provision.[35] In this instance, "sight" reflects power. From v. 1 it was clear that God was the same one setting the stage for the entire horrific episode; it was God who envisioned this final "test."

The Stay of Execution

To this point, the journey has been long and fraught with implicit fear and uncertainty.[36] Given the limited information at their disposal, surely neither Abraham nor Isaac looked with eagerness to the destination. The place that only God could see in the first instance is now before them. Vv. 9–10 are words of terror. For those of us who have witnessed a cremation, where a pyre is built and a body placed on it and then set ablaze, these verses are horrific. There is an extraordinary feeling that engulfs the human system as one watches a body burned to ashes, though the body be a lifeless corpse. How much more the thought of a living person? Abraham knowingly, willingly, systematically prepares to kill his son! The fact that there was precedence for child sacrifice in the Ancient Near East and the Hebrew tradition neither justifies nor elevates its moral acceptability.

The angel's call to Abraham sounds a note of urgency in the repetition of the name. Abraham's response continues as before—the standard *hinneni*! Does Abraham know or sense the outcome? Does Abraham resign himself? Is he simply numbed by the circumstances and dutifully executes his functions? The element of distance is again reinforced as the domain of the angel is in heaven and from there comes the call. On the other hand textual reference to the divine domain demonstrates assurance that God is aware of, and involved in terrestrial matters. In v. 12, the words of the angel connect *naʿar*, *ben*, and *yachîd*. With the provision of a ram for the sacrifice, the language of distance converges with the language of closeness. The spatial language

---

35. Brueggemann refers to Karl Barth's novel idea of connecting "provide" to the Latin *pro-video*, *Genesis*, 189–90. This imaginative rendering captures the essence of God's power. This is a God who not only sees that which is immediately in the present, but one who pierces the future with a vision that is out of reach of humans.

36. See Auerbach, *Mimesis*. Auerbach observes that, "The journey is like a silent process through the indeterminate and the contingent, a holding of the breath, a process which has no present, which is inserted like a blank duration, between what has passed and what lies ahead," 10.

of distance and separation in vv. 3–4 alerts us to the distancing between the sacrificer and the one to be sacrificed.

The silence and lack of resistance on the part of Isaac are astonishing. If nothing else, has this one without voice and power given up hope and resigns himself to death? One must wonder what went through the very heart of Isaac. What does it mean to trust one's parent and know that one could be killed by that parent under the guise of faithfulness to God? Could this experience strengthen the faith of Isaac or destroy his level of trust?[37] From a dramatic perspective there is nothing more spellbinding and chilling than an eleventh hour rescue from the jaws of death. But this narrative is not meant to be such a spectacle. When the angel finally stops Abraham one instantly wants to celebrate and shout for joy. Yet this very act does not build trust and faith, but indebtedness. The language of indebtedness is the language of enslavement.[38]

If there were any doubt as to the domain of the highest level of power, vv. 11–12 erase any such question. At the eleventh hour in the face of such an horrific act, God intervenes. Taken in isolation, the angel's words are indeed words of life in the face of death. Yet, as the narrative leads us, one must repeatedly ask, on behalf of the silent Isaac and the absent Sarah: "why the request in the first place?" "Fear of God" is the conclusion drawn after the eleventh hour rescue. The implication is that to challenge God in the light of such a horrifying "test" would be disobedient. Soelle, who sees this climactic moment in v. 12 differently, concludes, "It was not a matter of choosing between two conflicting values or, to put it in ancient terms, between two gods, but only between the fear of God and disobedience. The test was whether Abraham feared and loved God above all things."[39] As logical and perhaps even reasonable as this might

37. Wiesel pursues further other theological questions. "If God needs human suffering to be God, how can man foresee an end to that suffering? And if faith in God must result in self-denial, how can faith claim to elevate and improve man?" "The Sacrifice of Isaac," 73.

38. Crenshaw concludes that, "Since God imposed the burden, no credit should accompany the removal of the heavy load." "A Monstrous Test," 12–13 n. 9. In seeking to justify the eleventh hour provision and the ensuing silence by both Abraham and Isaac, Breithart suggests, "The silent torment accompanying the resolution was the only answer as all deeply religious questions are," "The Akedah," 27.

39. Soelle, *Suffering*, 31. The complexity of the reasons for the test is seen in part through the many and varied opinions. Moster, "The Testing of Abraham," argues that, "Abraham passed the test with flying colors. The test did not prove that he was willing

appear, the reality is that it is profoundly problematic as we struggle to discern the nature of God. Abraham is praised for his willingness to give up his son, the very son who is the promise bearer. The detachment is lauded. In v. 12b, it is clear that the sacrifice was more for God's sake than anyone else's. "You have not withheld your son—from me." That is the issue. Thus it is not so much Abraham's willingness to sacrifice as it is his willingness not to hold onto. Perhaps if there is a redemptive value in this type of testing, it is to ensure that one does not hold onto a treasure in an attempt to create an indistinguishable bonding, thereby suffocating its identity and robbing it of its life. The "test" is brutal, though the potential to hold onto also has death-like implications.[40]

Abraham's response after the sacrifice of the ram is confession. His confession in v. 14a *yhwh yir'eh* recalls his answer to Isaac in v. 8. While the confession comes on the heels of the eleventh hour provision, the use of *yhwh yir'eh* in v. 14a helps us understand the openness of the response in v. 8. The vision ascribed to God is one which spans the future and there are neither spatial nor temporal boundaries. The use of the future tense (*yr'h*) clearly speaks not only to the provision of the ram, but what might be sought in the future.

Where Is Isaac?

At one level, we are led to conclude that vv. 15–18 constitute a reiteration of the promise made to Abraham in Gen. 12:1–4. While there are

---

to sacrifice his son. It was not a test of 'obedience.' On the contrary, it was a test of 'faith' in God's promise," 241. See also Moberly who sees definitive tension between "testing" and "fearing God," a tension which he argues is critical for an understanding of Exod. 20:20. "...The overarching concern of the story is God's test of Abraham (v. 1) which is completely resolved by Abraham's obedience. (v. 12) The meaning of this is illuminated when it is appreciated that the two key words, test (*nissah*) and fear (*yare'*) occur in conjunction in one other context of fundamental theological importance that is Exod. 20:20. Here it is explained that God has given Israel his Torah, supremely the test commandments, to test (*nissah*) them so that the fear (*yir'ah*) of God should be before them so that they do not sin," *Eden to Golgotha*, 57.

40. A useful analogy is articulated by Breech who proposes that the person, "who puts his hand to the plow and looks back is someone who has to 'hold on' to what he is doing in order to know its value. The image, then, is one of lack of confidence, an absence of a non-reflective awareness of the value of what he is doing . . . The image of the man who puts his hand to the plow and looks back identifies a particular mode of being human from its distinctive mode of *consciousness*, which is a *holding* mode," *The Silence of Jesus*, 46.

certainly common elements, there are also notable differences. Coming on the heels of the provision of the ram, and the sparing of Isaac's life, the promise is now couched in language of condition. It is because (*kî*) of Abraham's willingness to release Isaac that Yahweh will indeed bless him. It is difficult to separate the acknowledgment of Abraham's obedience (v. 16) and the use of the infinitive absolute form of *brk*. Prior to this, the narrative never hinted at the promise being conditional and there is no further discussion within the narrative of this new element.[41] The singular voice of God dominates the scene and further testifies to the intentionality of the narrator's focus on power structure. Indeed, for the rest of this narrative, the voices of Abraham and Isaac are silent!

As it began, the narrative ends on a note of difficulty. Where is Isaac? As the narrative concludes, it is Abraham who returns (*vayšav*) together with the servants. The text provides sufficient inferences that after the ordeal, the relationship between Abraham and Isaac became irreparably strained. There are at least four textual examples that underline such a conclusion. First, the absence of any reference to Isaac returning with Abraham suggests that perhaps Abraham and Isaac separated. It is Abraham who returned, and Abraham who lived at Beer-Sheba. We recall that in v. 5 it was Abraham who assured the servants that "we shall return."

Second, after the Akedah experience Abraham and Isaac are never again in conversation with each other. Textually, the intent is to suggest that both relational and geographical separation had taken place between Isaac and Abraham. The next time that Isaac would be with Abraham is after Abraham's death. There is no mention of Isaac's presence at Sarah's funeral. The absence of any mention of Isaac at Sarah's death is particularly troubling as throughout the narrative, prior to the "testing" in Genesis 22, the closeness between Isaac and Sarah is pronounced. Speaking specifically in reference to the "test," Trible notes the illogical nature of the textual movement. Her words are equally apropos to the issue at hand. "Attachment is Sarah's problem. Nevertheless, Genesis 22 drops Sarah to insert Abraham. The switch defies the internal logic of the larger story. In view of the unique status of Sarah, and her exclusive relationship to Isaac, she, not Abraham ought to have

---

41. Sarna comments that, "All previous blessings are pure acts of divine grace; now for the first time, they are presented as a reward for Abraham's devotion to God," *Genesis*, 154.

been tested."⁴² Symbolically, to the extent that unity is an expression of life, Isaac and Abraham are united after the latter's death. Indeed Isaac comes from Beer-lahai-roi, the very place that Hagar in her own wilderness experience named for the God who saw her affliction.

Third, throughout Abraham's instructions to his oldest servant (Genesis 24) regarding the search for a suitable wife for Isaac, he never refers to Isaac by name, implying a continuing distance between father and son. There is no note in the text that Isaac was in fact present during this time. While Abraham seeks to execute his duty in securing a suitable wife for Isaac, Abraham's involvement is minimal and the servant's role further underlines the estrangement. When Isaac and Rebekah meet each other for the first time, remarkably there is no mention of Abraham. Perhaps under any circumstances, Abraham's absence would be surprising, but in this instance it is even more so, given the fact that he is the one who orchestrated the plans to secure a wife for Isaac, and the further reality that he had the role of a single parent since the death of Sarah. Indeed the narrative invites us to enter into the chambers of Isaac's grief.⁴³ He has not had the appropriate companion with whom to share the grief that he bore for Sarah. In Rebekah he found comfort, and it is to Sarah's tent (Gen. 24:67) that Rebekah is brought.

Fourth, at the death of Abraham, Isaac is blessed by God (Gen 25:11). One is left to wonder why it is that Abraham does not bless Isaac, an act so very typical of fathers and sons within the biblical tradition. Indeed, Isaac does not seek a blessing from his father. The journey will continue from a point of estrangement and brokenness.

---

42. Trible, "Genesis 22," 189.

43. Kohn raises the question as to whether the "Bible's silence regarding Isaac's daily conduct suggest that he suffered constant depressive and melancholic moods that caused him to avoid social intercourse, and to spend his time in solitude," "The Trauma of Isaac," 100.

6

Answering Violence with Violence

Judges 19

> "There may be times when we are powerless to prevent injustice, but there must never be a time a when we fail to protest."
> —Elie Wiesel

SCHOLARS GENERALLY RECOGNIZE THE SIMILARITY BETWEEN GENESIS 19 and Judges 19, and while there is, doubtless, an important connection, enough differences exist in theme, structure, and the subtleties of the narrative thereby qualifying these two texts for separate discussion.[1]

---

1. Westermann, *Genesis 12–36*, 297, provides a useful comparison between these texts.

Judges		Genesis
	arrival and reception	
19:15–21		19:1–3
	attack and repulse of attack	
19:22–25		19:4–11
	demand to hand over	
19:22		19:4–5
	offer by householder	
19:23–24		19:6–8
	rejection and threat	
19:25a		19:9
	repulse of attack by guests	
19:25b		19:10–11

This is a general comparison, and while it places before the readers the elements that connect these texts, it does not in any way explore in detail many of the differences that in fact do exist. See Niditch, "The 'Sodomite' Theme," 375, who concludes that, "one cannot reach a definitive conclusion about the relationship between the two passages." See also, Lasine, "Guest and Host in Judges 19"; and Matthews, "Hospitality

Judges 19 has to be considered in its entirety in order to understand fully the events in Gibeah between the Levite and the men of that land. The critical constituent in this episode surrounds the role of the woman. It is true that the name of neither the Levite nor the woman is given, though we are told of the tribal identity of the man, namely that he is from the tribe of Levi. This designation is one of the elements the text provides by way of giving an identity to the man. Even such minimal identity designation aids in creating a sharper differentiation between the man and the woman[2] as no clues are offered concerning the identity of the woman.[3] Not only does she remain anonymous throughout the text, but together with her anonymity, she is typically spoken of in connection with two men in her life, her husband and her father.[4]

---

and Hostility in Genesis 19 and Judges 19." Also, Gaiser, "Homosexuality and the Old Testament," 163, observes that "the Sodom story and the Gibeah story must be read together. The outrage in the latter case is even greater since the offense is perpetrated by members of the covenant community. Sexual violence cannot be ascribed only to others. Nor can it be limited to homosexual activity. It is the heterosexual abuse of a woman which brings God's judgment in Gibeah, paralleling the judgment of attempted homosexual abuse of men at Sodom."

2. See Martin, *The Book of Judges*, 199. Contra Soggin, *Judges*, who argues that this designation of "Levite" is unimportant for this narrative. Also Jungling, *Richter 19*, who argues that this title be removed from the text entirely. On the importance of naming, Fretheim, *The Suffering of God*, 99–100, acknowledges that, "Naming entails life. Names are given to those who are living . . . Naming entails distinctiveness, setting one off from others who have names. God gives God's name and thereby is set off from other gods who have names . . . Moreover naming entails a certain kind of relationship. Giving the name opens up the possibility of, indeed admits a desire for, a certain intimacy in relationship. A relationship without a name inevitably means some distance. Naming the name is necessary for closeness. Fretheim's idea on the importance of naming, particularly with respect to intimacy and relationship, is piercing in both its truth and applicability to the anonymous woman.

3. See Mabee, *Reimagining America*. Speaking specifically with regard to *Moby-Dick*, the author underlines the importance of naming. Without the name to provide identity, Mabee argues that the name would be nothing more than an adventure story. "It is the known identity of Moby-Dick that gives the story theological meaning," ibid., 70. Yet, in the Judges story, even with the anonymity of the woman, perhaps precisely because of her anonymity, one is impelled to confront the theological nucleus. This nucleus will be approached from the margin, which is the common abode of the anonymous and marginalized.

4. Trible, *Texts of Terror*, 66, notes that the Levite right from the start is clearly set up as the subject and the woman as the object.

According to the narrator, the reason for her return to her father's house has to do with her "playing the harlot" against her husband.[5] Most English translations render this phrase as pertaining to the woman's anger at her husband.[6] However it is instructive to note the similarity between the reference here and that which we find in Hosea 2.

Hosea 2	Judges 19
v. 7 [v. 5] *kî zantah*	v. 2 *vatizneh*
v. 6 [v. 16] *v^edibbartî ʿal-libbah*	v. 3 *l^edabber ʿal-libbah*

Gomer is described as having "played the harlot." In the Hosea text, there is little doubt that the metaphor of harlotry is used as a way of talking about the brokenness in the relationship between God and Israel. The issue which Hosea addresses has to do with the rejection of the covenantal love. To be sure the incident in the Judges' text does not involve the relationship between God and the people as the main focus, but it does involve a formal relationship, as in the case between a man and a woman.

On one level it would appear that the woman is the one who is to be blamed for this separation. If we take the MT text as is and proceed to form conclusions on this basis, the separation might be attributed to the woman, for she is described as the one who has prostituted herself. Moreover, she is the one who left her husband[7] and returned to her

---

5. This is one of only two instances in the text (the other being v. 26, where she chooses where to die!) where a decision is made by the woman. In every other instance, the woman's fate is determined by the man. It is the discussion between her father and the Levite that determines whether or not she will return and it is the Levite who decides when to leave her father's house. The Levite and the servant boy are the ones who decide where to spend the night and finally it is the decision of the old man and the Levite to give the women in place of the Levite for the men of Gibeah to rape.

6. There are two extant manuscript traditions that take the text in different directions. Both the MT and the Syriac read, "his concubine played the harlot," while the Greek and the Old Latin read, "his concubine became angry with him." For a discussion of these traditions, see Soggin, *Judges*, 284. Boling, *Judges*, 273–74. Also, Klein, *The Triumph of Irony in the Book of Judges*, 232 n. 6, argues that "the ambiguity of the Hebrew reinforces the bride-whore-idolatry motif recurrent in Judges, and implicitly faults the Levite for not adhering to covenantal law, thus preparing for the development of his character in the narrative."

7. This is the only time when "husband" is used as describing the man's relation to the woman. The Hebrew term employed here is ʾîšah, which the narrator alerts us to, precisely because it sets the stage for an understanding of the nature of the relationship, despite the manner in which the woman is treated later. See also, de Vaux, *Ancient*

father's house. Given this, the fact that the Levite comes for her and speaks tenderly posits him in a light that is very flattering and full of grace, at least at this point. After all, if it is the woman who is to be blamed for the brokenness in the relationship, then the actions of the Levite are extraordinarily graceful. Again, this would certainly parallel the Hosea story, for it is Hosea who goes after Gomer when she re-enters the world of harlotry.

However, there are elements in this text that allow us to see that it is not entirely like this. We must ask the question, "why?" Why would this woman leave her husband? From all indications he is wealthy; the possession of a concubine in and of itself denotes wealth. It is the woman's actions which lead us to the new reality that relationships cannot only be predicated on the degree of comfort brought by the resource of wealth. If wealth were the only or even the central factor in determining a relationship, then the woman's actions would have been much more problematic. The reality is that she would profit more if she went after other lovers as in fact Gomer did. But this woman did not go after other lovers according to the narrative. If indeed we are to take seriously the phrase *vatizneh*, then we must by necessity move beyond simply the pursuit of lovers as an appropriate interpretation. The process of prostituting oneself in this text only makes proper sense when understood in the light of breaking certain fundamental expectations of a relationship. It would appear that the woman takes the relationship between herself and the Levite so seriously, that leaving her husband might very well be considered prostitution of the relationship. If anything, it is the woman who is noble in her actions at this point.[8] She appears to be the one intent on fulfilling and receiving all the expectations of a relationship. There is no indication that the woman used her father's house as the base of an operation for prostitution. The confusion here has prompted some interpreters to predicate their hermeneutic on the basis of anger by the woman. That the woman was angry certainly has basis in the

---

Israel, 26, notes that in a typical Israelite marriage, "The husband is called the *baʿal* or 'master' of his wife, just as he is the *baʿal* of a house or field . . . A married woman is therefore the 'possession' of her *baʿal*." See, e.g., Exod 21:3.

8. See the NIV, which translates v. 2a: "But she was unfaithful to him." This rendering takes the MT in a very superficial way and thereby misses the deeper essence of the narrator's intent. The *Tanakh* renders it, "she deserted him," and the NJB, "In a fit of anger."

story, but there are two other integral factors that direct the path of interpretation.

First, the man takes four months to return to the woman. By itself one might take this period of time as an indication of the man's reluctance to accept the woman again because of her actions, if indeed unfaithfulness were the issue. Though the narrator fails to articulate the precise issue, we know that the man was reluctant to go after the woman immediately after her departure.

Second, lest we rely solely on deductions to determine the direction of the narrator's intent, we are told that finally it is the husband who seeks the woman and comes to her and speaks "from the heart." It is the Levite who comes in repentance and seeks to have the woman re-enter the relationship. On the surface, the fact that the man is the one who seeks out the woman, might suggest that this is an admission of wrongdoing in the first place. Again, this is not explicit in the text. However, the use of the Hebrew root *šûb* in v. 3 implies that the "return" of the woman is not only a reference to the hope of physical reunion of the Levite and the woman, but given the intent to "speak tenderly," it seems that "return" in this context alludes also to the hope that the woman might again be emotionally inclined to be in relationship with him.[9] Using the Hosea text as a guide here, we recall that "speaking from the heart" was a point in which a renewed effort was being made to sustain the relationship. All indications point to a hope for a new beginning: considerable time had elapsed since the separation between the two; the woman has been away at her father's house and the Levite has had significant time for reflection.

What of the Woman?

The time spent under the hospitable care of the father-in-law provides significant insights into the manner of acceptable and unacceptable hospitality. The man is greeted with joy by the father. The initial invitation by the woman's father is not all that unusual as he invites the husband and his servant to spend three days. What is immediately

---

9. See Trible, *Texts of Terror*, 67, who notes that, "The Levite's speaking to the heart of his concubine indicates love for her without specifying guilt. The narrative censures no one for the concubine's departure. Moreover, it portrays the master sympathetically. Be the woman innocent or guilty, he seeks reconciliation."

striking here is the virtual absence of the woman in the greeting, albeit that she is the one who admits the Levite in. The irony of the entire event is that the woman is the reason why the man returned to this place and throughout the engagement the woman is absent, certainly in voice.[10] Marginality is manifestly demonstrated. In many arenas of life, it is noticeable that the marginalized often have voices stifled. Surely the woman in this story is one who is marginalized.[11] A repulsive element here is emphasized by the narrator, for there is little doubt that the woman is being taken for granted.[12] In essence, the entire interlude at the father's house exemplifies the dismantling of one's personhood through indifference. The reality is that this is an early indication of what is to come, for surely, indifference leads inexorably to death.

The relationship with the woman is never in these verses a point of discussion. We cannot argue from absence here and assume that the father is glad because his daughter was wrong in the first place. Throughout the Levite's stay at the woman's house, the latter is never a part of the conversation. In fact she is never given the choice: to remain with her father or return with her husband. To this point the narrator gives no indication that the woman was in the least interested in the continued relationship with the man. The narrator rather notes that the man came and spoke tenderly (from the heart) and the woman on this basis responded favorably; at least, there is no suggestion in the text of reluctance on her part. On the one hand, there is really no reason here to dispute the integrity of the man, for speaking from the heart would indicate that he is in fact seeking to be honest. However, one cannot overlook the response of the woman. In responding the way she did, the intentionality of the narrative is made clear. This woman is perfectly capable of distinguishing between that which is true and honest and that

---

10. Ibid., The switch from a plural to a singular pronoun, from *they* to *he*, shows that the woman is not counted in either verb (68).

11. See Brueggemann, "Canonization and Contextualization," 128. While the oppressed have typically looked to Deut 26:7 as a credo by which to live, it is apparent that within the casting of those who are oppressed, there are those who are marginalized. In the case of the woman in this story, one must wonder what is necessary for her voice to be heard by one who has promised deliverance or at least attentive ears to the cries of the distressed.

12. See Trible, *Texts of Terror*, 68, who observes regarding the Levite and the father-in-law that, "as these two unite, the woman who brought them together fades from the scene. Truly this version of oriental hospitality is an exercise in male bonding."

which is deceitful. With this in mind the description that the woman prostituted herself opens to us the valid possibility of this woman pursuing that which is sure and founded on more than societal norms. The fact of the matter is that a concubine is assumed to have similar rights as a married person. A woman "walking out" on her husband would on one level appear to be unacceptable behavior and in this fashion be considered harlotry. However, on a much deeper and life-giving level, the action of the woman maintains the essential ingredient necessary for a relationship between a man and a woman, namely intimacy. In the eyes of the society it might be considered harlotry to leave one's spouse. However, the lack of intimacy is much more problematic, and often, this void in a relationship is given little attention. This anonymous woman opened the way for people of all time to know that one need not settle only for that which society has determined acceptable. In the silence of the woman, she establishes a new height by which relationships might be based. Consider the extraordinary situation: a woman with little or no status in society, risks everything, including a potential for death, as she pursues integrity and truth.[13]

The text uses four different Hebrew terms to describe the woman. The term *naʿarah* is used no less than six times and all of them in the interlude at her father's house. This word translated as "girl," "damsel," or such is meant to stress the fact she was a young person. But, there is another element to note here. The narrator cleverly uses this term to plant three ideas in the minds of readers. First, this term does not imply any kind of marital obligations, and while she is at her father's house, there is a sense that the woman is still undecided as to whether she will be reunited with the Levite. As long as she was in her father's house, she remained a *naʿarah*. To be sure, this indicates the manner in which the narrator speaks about her while with her father, but more importantly, she is perceived to be one who, though young, will in fact take some time to decide her future.

Second, by using this term, we are invited to draw a parallel between the *naʿar*, the servant boy and the woman. Even though the language alerts us to this connection, this young woman would be treated

---

13. See Klein, *The Triumph of Irony in the Book of Judges*, 163, who parallels both the Levite's and the woman's behavior with the pronouncement that "everyone did what was right in their eyes." "The consequences of her actions are an implicit judgment of her as well as her husband."

with less dignity than the servant. To be sure her life will be given less value than that of the *naʿarah*.

Three other Hebrew terms are used to describe the woman in relation to the Levite. In v. 19, the term *velaʾamateka* is employed as the Levite accepts the invitation of the old man and introduces the members of his entourage. The fact that *ʾamah* is conventionally rendered "handmaid" gives some indication of the presumed role of the concubine.[14] In the introductory section of the narrative (vv. 1–2) we are introduced to her as *tizneh*, the concubine of the Levite. This term is not used again until after they departed from her father's house. (v. 9) While the term certainly has overtones of marital responsibility, the reality is that the concubine is treated precisely as a concubine. Twice, (vv. 26, 27) the narrator uses *ʾiššah* to refer to the woman. These are the only instances in the text where this term is used and at one level it appears that it is ill used. While *ʾiššah* is generally translated "woman," the direction of the narrative would warrant a rendering of "wife."[15] In a way, the narrator points to the transformation of the *naʿarah* into an *ʾiššah*. When the woman return to the threshold of the house after she is abused and raped, she is referred to as the *ʾiššâh* of the Levite. The responsibility of the Levite is precisely more pronounced here.[16]

Freedom of the Visitor

There is no question that the father knew the man when he arrived at the house. Whether it is on this basis that hospitality is demonstrated one cannot be sure. However, there is undeniable hospitality shown to

---

14. The use of *ʾamah* here signals in no uncertain terms something of the approaching violence. By way of placing this reference in context, *ʾamah* is also the term used of Hagar in Gen 21:10; of Bilhah in Gen 30:3; and of the women slaves in Gen 20:17. Particularly in the case of Hagar and Bilhah, they are both used (or intended to be used) for sexual purposes and then discarded. That *ʾamah* is used here of the concubine signals tragedy for her.

15. One is summoned by the narrator to recall the parallelism between the use of *ʾiššah* in these instances and the use of *ʾiššah* in v. 3. Speiser notes however, that *ʾiššah* may be rendered as either "wife" or "concubine," reflecting the cognate associations in other ancient Near Eastern languages, 117.

16. See Klein, *The Triumph of Irony in the Book of Judges*, 170, who makes an interesting observation noting that the person who left the house of the old man was a *naʿarah* and the person who returned was an *ʾiššah*. According to Klein the change in terms here points to the bitter irony.

the man and his servant; to be sure three days is common practice, but it is pushed beyond this. Particularly as one reflects carefully on vv. 3–9 one cannot help but be struck by the continued high level of hospitality on the part of the father. Yet, there is a flaw in this attitude as we enter into the scenario somewhat more closely. The dignity of the visitor is slowly erased under the guise of provision. Though the father had provided abundantly for the man and his servant, he nevertheless insisted that they remain, first for an extra day and yet another day. Essential to the act of hospitality is the ability and the readiness of the host to allow the visitor to continue on the journey. It is simply not a part of the biblical notion of hospitality, that food and drink be offered as incentives for visitors to remain longer than desired or necessary in a particular place (see Gen 18:5).[17] The intent of the host is sharpened as we come to notice the narrator's emphasis on the eating and the drinking. Both in vv. 6 and 8 we are reminded that the Levite and the father are the ones who are eating and drinking. While it is not unreasonable to surmise that the woman and the servant were also eating and drinking during this time, the focus is clearly on the two men. There are two components in vv. 3–9 that merit attention.

First, the catalogue of verbs used in these verses testifies to the pressure exerted on the guests to remain longer than they wished, as well as the reality that there was little to accomplish by remaining longer:

> made him stay (v. 4)
>
> urged him strongly (v. 7)
>
> they lingered; the day declined (v. 8).

The Hebrew verb used in v. 7 is *pṣr* which has the connotation of pressing someone against his/her will. This is also the verb which is found in Gen 19:3 where Lot insists on the visitors staying with him, and also in Gen 19:9b where the men of Sodom are described as "pressing hard" against Lot. This term has less than positive overtones. The presence of a term such as this with respect to the father gives a clue as the motivation of the father. The entire time spent at the father's house would

---

17. Contra Klein, ibid., 164, who argues that this episode between the father and the Levite helps to establish the inconsiderate nature of the Levite. "Under the circumstances, the fact that the Levite stays beyond the conventional three days certainly imposes hardship upon the economics of the host family. The character of the Levite—that he is selfish and inconsiderate of others—emerges from his overstay."

have to come under scrutiny because of the ulterior motives which are captured by *pṣr*.

Second, the use of the Hebrew *lav* creates a multi-layered meaning in the text. As we have noted before, the reference to the tenderness of the man in the seeking after the woman has to do principally with the fact that his intentions are from the heart. The heart would serve as that which is of paramount importance in the potential to change the situation. We are led to believe by the narrator that the heart is the premier force behind newness and change.[18] It is the function of the heart that allows for decision-making. Reason, logic and other forms of intellectual bases are not of consequence here; it is the heart which takes center stage.[19] With this in mind, the narrator cleverly uses this term for the host to persuade the guest to change his mind. The term *lav* is used in four instances between vv. 5–9. Twice the NRSV translates the term "fortify" (vv. 5, 8) and twice renders *lav* "enjoy" (vv. 6, 9).[20]

An Essential Tension

The entire interlude spent at the house of the woman was devoted to the father and the husband. The structure of these verses underlines the discourse between these two men and the father's insistence on the husband remaining longer than necessary. These verses are critical for an understanding of the overall issues in the narrative. When the husband finally decides to take his leave, only here is the woman mentioned, and then only in passing. To this point there was no indication from the narrator that the woman would be conspicuously absent from all the deliberations. The woman is never given the opportunity to discuss or respond, and clearly there is no indication given in the text that the issues which led to the separation in the first instance have been attended

18. While the context is different, the use of *lav* in other instances such as Jer 31:33 affirm the heart as the center for newness and change. Moreover, there is something about decisions made from the heart that point to a degree of permanence.

19. In this regard, reflection on the actions of Ruth in accompanying Naomi is instructive. While the actions of Orpah are sensible and under the circumstances reasonable and logical, Ruth's actions are borne neither out of reason nor logic. Rather, she acts from the heart and makes a decision based on compassion.

20. See the RSV, which makes clear that *lav* is followed somewhat more closely by rendering these occurrences as "strengthening of the heart" and "merriment of the heart." The NIV renders these as "refresh yourself" and "enjoy yourself."

to or resolved. Nevertheless she is on her way and the husband's quest has been fulfilled.

Before this however, the literary movement in the text establishes an identity of the woman which inverts not only the common expectations of the society, but also the established role of the woman. While the focus is on the men in vv. 3–9, it is noteworthy that throughout this section both men gain part of their identity from the woman. The father and husband are described in relationship to the woman.

> her husband (v. 3)
> the girl's father (v. 3)
> his father-in-law; the girl's father (v. 4)
> the girl's father (v. 5)
> the girl's father (v. 6)
> his father-in-law (v. 7)
> the girl's father (v. 8)
> his father-in-law; the girl's father (v. 9)

Prior to the husband's arrival, the woman is described as "his concubine" (vv. 1–2) and then as they are about to leave the father's house, she is again established as "his" concubine. (v. 9)[21]

The narrator establishes that the relationship between the man and the woman is likely a marital relationship. Given this, there are expectations on the part of both partners. Whether the father is identified as the "girl's father" or "his father-in-law," the reality is that he is identified through the woman. In vv. 4 and 9, the narrator goes to exhaustive lengths to emphasize the identity of the father through the woman. As if to establish the personhood of the woman, the identification of "his father-in-law" and "the girl's father" are used alongside each other.

With all of this though, the insignificance of the woman in the text is sharply punctuated. As the journey resumes, the woman is mentioned in the same breath as the laden donkeys, indeed after the donkeys are mentioned. (v. 10) While it is established that the reason

---

21. Trible, *God and the Rhetoric of Sexuality*, 191, observes the shifting of masculine pronouns to feminine pronouns in the opening verses of the book of Ruth. While the identity of both Naomi and Ruth is given shape here through this literary maneuver, later in 4:10 there is return to the way the narrative began, namely an emphasis on the man as the master and owner. "I have also acquired Ruth the Moabite, the wife of Mahlon, to be my wife" (4:10).

for the husband's trip to Bethlehem is to be reunited with the woman, as the journey begins, her presence is noted merely in passing.[22] It is interesting to note also, that while there is joy by the father on seeing the son-in-law, any such joy expressed by either the Levite or the woman on seeing each other is conspicuously absent.

The omission of any other member of the entourage is deafening in its implications. We know from both vv. 3 and 13 that there was a servant who accompanied the man. One is led to conclude that the woman, despite the importance which is placed upon her by her husband's journey to re-claim her, she is again treated as a property, in this case less in importance than servant, and the laden donkeys.[23] This is particularly striking because there is little doubt that the man had the financial capacity to have another concubine if all that mattered was having a woman who might be recognized as property. Arguably, this woman was unwilling to be placed in the category of property and consequently left. Together with this, the narrator's subtle insistence that this woman has rights akin to those of a spouse, makes the treatment of this woman at the resumption of the journey particularly problematic. One cannot miss the stark juxtaposition of the woman's unwavering belief that there are fundamental expectations borne out of a relationship such as this. She expressed concretely her independence in returning to Bethlehem and this is set against her notable silence, and the virtual textual silence as the Levite seeks her out for the purpose of renewing the relationship. It is this ongoing tension between freedom and authority that the narrator proposes in the juxtaposition of these seemingly incongruous positions. What transpires in vv. 1–9 sets the stage for the development of the journey and the ensuing encounter with the men of Gibeah.

---

22. See Tanakh, which renders this: "his concubine was *also* with him" (my italics). The translation captures the essence of the narrator's intent, for the literary disposition of the text suggests that the woman is something of an afterthought. The irony here naturally is that the woman must really be the central focus of the journey. Instead she is relegated to join the heavy-laden donkeys.

23. Klein, *The Triumph of Irony in the Book of Judges*, 169–70, suggests that the Levite, "pursues the concubine because he misses her (presumably sexually), but in masculine company—her father's presence or even that of his servant—he ignores her. The concubine is a sexual object, not worthy of speech, not 'human.'"

Shades of Darkness

On the heels of vv. 7–9a, in vv. 9b–16a, there are eight temporal references all of which have to do with evening or night. In v. 9b, even before the Levite leaves Bethlehem, the narrator establishes that "the day had drawn to a close." The Hebrew term used here is ʿereb, which reveals that it was already getting dark. Consequently, leaving Bethlehem a place of security, regardless of the intentions of the host, does not appear judicious. Nevertheless, the Levite together with the woman and the servant leave. By the time these travelers arrive in the city of the Jebusites, it was most certainly dark, for the Hebrew text reads, *hayom rad meʾod*, which if pursued as is, would indicate that the day was already far extended.[24] Yet, given this reality the man would not listen to the suggestion of the servant that they stop there for the night. Though night is descending and they are foreigners in the land, the proposition to find lodging is summarily dismissed with no discussion, and they continue on the journey. These references to darkness serve two different functions.

First, the end of the day brings with it a darkness which signals not only an end to a time of work and an advent of weariness, but also a time to stop and rest for the night.

Second, there is the metaphorical use which spotlights the myopic and bigoted nature of the Levite. The fact that he is willing to proceed in the midst of the darkness alerts us to his ability to dwell in the midst of darkness and not be at all troubled by it. We see several points of darkness on the trajectory of the Levite's life, thus noting that he is indeed living within the scope of deep darkness. One of the ironies here is that it is the servant who is willing to stop and rest regardless of the racial, cultural and religious identity of the residents of the city. The use of *naʿar* intensifies the Levite's shortsightedness.[25]

---

24. The Hebrew text here is not at all clear and while most English translations readily settle for a rendering such as, "the day was far spent," there are other positions that have been taken. In the regard, the NEB translates this phrase as, "the weather grew wild and stormy." If we were to follow the NEB, it would testify further to the necessity of spending the night in the Jebusite city.

25. One notes an important parallel between the *naʿar* and the *naʿarah naʿar* which occurs in this narrative's suggestion that it is the *naʿar* who, on noticing the blanket of darkness seeks to find a place of rest and break away from the present direction. In the case of the relationship between the *naʿarah* and the Levite, perhaps it is her perception, that, because of the pervading darkness, a new direction was necessary. It is no surprise that all six occasions in which *naʿarah* is used in this narrative, are found

The only reason given by the Levite for continuing the journey by dark is that he has no desire to "turn aside into a city of foreigners, who do not belong to the people of Israel" (19:12). Consider the undeniable element of exclusivity and separatism here. Employing the many temporal references noted above, the narrator impresses upon us the extremity of the Levite's disdain (and fear?) of foreigners and strangers. The Levite is intent on sojourning with his own. The Hebrew term *nokri* is used to refer to the Jebusites and this is set in sharp contradistinction to the Israelite regardless whether the latter was a citizen or a sojourner (*ger*) as in fact both the Levite (v. 1) and the old man (v. 16) were.[26]

But there is a further issue at stake here. Essential to the covenantal relationship with Yahweh is the fact that the Israelites are to be a blessing to others. Reading this text, one is mindful of the promises pronounced in Genesis 12, inclusive of the one that Abraham is to be a blessing to others. Without ever giving the Jebusites a chance for blessing they are rejected on the basis on their status as strangers. Two expressions of apparent danger are implied here. The more explicit of the two has to do with the suspicion and the fear of the *nokri*.[27] The narrator provides no reason or explanation for this attitude, but in the absence of such, establishes the fact this was very much part of the make-up of the covenant people: a prevalent phobia borne out of distrust and difference. But this was only part of the issue. The actions of the Levite had overtones of significant gravity that went beyond simply a matter of paranoia or preference. In addition to not trusting the *nokri*, he also effectively eliminated any opportunity of receiving hospitality by a rank outsider. Can there be a good and hospitable Jebusite? By summarily dismissing the suggestion of the servant-boy, the Levite slammed the door on any such possibility. Moreover, the Levite's attitude towards the

---

within the context of her father's house. While her father's house was not an entirely new direction, it is certainly a change from the house of the Levite.

26. See Gamoran, "The Biblical Law against Loans on Interest," 130, who notes that the *nokri* is "the foreigner who came to the land for a limited period of time, and the *ger*, the alien who permanently settled among the Israelites." Also, Neufeld, "The Prohibitions against Loans at Interest in Ancient Hebrew Laws," 389, who notes that, "The *nokri* stood in no relation to the tribe and could claim no legal rights; . . . he had neither home nor right in Israel."

27. This idea is hardly new, for it is this fear of the foreigner which prompts Abraham to pawn Sarah off as his sister (Genesis 12; 20). Not only is this an ignoble act, it takes away from the opportunity to be a blessing to others.

servant-boy displays a lack of hospitality. This restrictive and narrow perspective is further underlined as the evening gave way to the darkness of the night.

In distressing ways, the attitude of the Levite reflects certain attitudes of contemporary believers.[28] It is easier to trust those who share similar ideals and beliefs. This orientation spills over readily into the political arena. Those who are "non-believers" are often viewed with suspicion and the establishment of relationships are invariably predicated on changing the "other" to have him or her take the shape of the familiar, whether in religious or political ideology.[29] Active proselytizing is not an uncommon activity among well meaning believers who are utterly incapable of removing themselves from a level of suspicion of "outsiders." But could there be anything good among Muslims, Hindus, Buddhists, Ninevites, Canaanites? Could there be anything good in a socialist or communist system? Simply to ask these questions, seeking honest answers; willing to listen; willing to risk being changed by the dialogue; willing to admit to recognizing truth in another, or the "other," without having a foregone conclusion would be a step in the right direction in seeking to understand what it means to be hospitable.[30]

These questions are not academic questions *per se*, but in light of this text they have to be pursued for their effect on life. Constitutive of the reaction of the Levite is the apparent security one feels in the midst of the familiar. Brueggemann correctly points out an important, life-giving tension: "To stay in safety is to remain barren; to leave in risk is to have hope."[31] Here, Brueggemann suggests in effect that trust, even of the unknown and the different, is essential for newness and life. The Levite would choose to do otherwise. Perhaps one might say that

28. Brueggemann, *Genesis*, 112, concludes that, "the ideology of pride...presume[s] that the world is essentially a human artifact, that all possibilities are comprehended in human capacities for good or for ill."

29. For a helpful discussion of these matters, see Suchocki, "In Search of Justice."

30. See DeJong, *The Wheel on the School*, 6, who with insight and simplicity in a perspective addressed to children, catches the attention of adults also when he says, "For sometimes when we wonder, we can make things begin to happen."

31. Brueggemann, *Genesis*, 118. Also, speaking to the security and privatization of the group dynamics of the religious establishment of Jesus' time, Breech, *The Silence of Jesus*, 27, opines, "The group psychology which governs the reactions of Jesus' contemporaries is identical to that of a group of children playing games who resent those who refuse to submit to the rules that control the activities of the group. Those individuals who refuse to be tribalized are treated as defectors."

the Levite was incapacitated by his own restricted notion of goodness, by whom it might be mediated, and to whom it might be attributed. Therefore, despite the immanent onset of darkness and the possibility of inclement weather, safety demanded dwelling among those familiar to him. The terse dismissal sets the stage for the intent of the narrator. The irony is that the Levite and his entourage settle in the town square, the central location in the city with the natural hope that they would be invited in by a citizen of the city. No one does!

The old man returning from the field is the only one to show any kind of hospitality, and as if to punctuate further the irony, he is described as one who was sojourning (*gar*) in Gilead and hailed from the "hill country of Ephraim," the place of origin of the Levite. Note the striking contrast between the two: initially, the old man does not know the identity of the visitor, clearly indicated by the use of "wayfarer," yet, he is openly hospitable to this stranger. Here, we are reminded that not all people manifest inhospitable attitude. The narrative reinforces the reality that the Levite is shunned by those he considered as covenantal kins. To be sure the darkness of night had fallen by the time they arrived in Gibeah. By itself this suggests that the travelers might not have been seen by the people of Gibeah. On the contrary, however, as we shall see, the people not only saw the Levite, but plotted against him.

Double Violence

The Levite, the woman and the servant were all invited to rest in the house of the old man.[32] All that one would expect by way of hospitality is given to the guests; and it is within the process of having their hearts satisfied that some men of the city came to the old man's house, demanding that the old man send the Levite out so that they might get to know (*yada'*) him.[33] The connotation here is generally considered sexual.[34]

---

32. Many Hebrew manuscripts together with the Vulgate and the Targum carry the singular "your servant" (v. 19). This is the preferred reading, as it fits the narrative better. The Levite's intention is to take care of himself and even the self-deprecation here alludes to his selfish motives.

33. The irony and tragedy here is that the old man who has a female guest, and must under the circumstances afford her hospitality, places her at the disposal of the Gibeah men to be raped and killed. See Trible, *Texts of Terror*, 75.

34. In fact the NRSV translates *yada'* in the text as "intercourse" while in a similar context in Gen 19:5, it is rendered "know."

However some elements in this text raise critical questions that are not germane to the Genesis 19 text. There is little doubt from this episode that the men of Gibeah are aware that the woman and the servant boy have entered the house of the man and they specifically sought to have the Levite come out to them. The narrator indicates that the men were of ill repute, and their request for the Levite was enveloped in evil intentions. The impression of the old man is that these men of the city were evil and they were seeking to have sexual relations with the Levite and thus he refused to have the Levite go out. One is naturally led to ask why the men of the city did not also demand the servant boy. After all, if it is sexual relations with a man that they were seeking, then surely the young boy would also have been a target. But in fact the servant never enters into this scenario. The intense and violent nature of these men is introduced in v. 22 through three points: (1) they are perditious men; (2) they pounded on the door of the house; (3) the use of *yada'* suggests that their intent was hardly noble and if anything it was sinister. The narrator effectively makes the danger known.[35]

Though the old man is a *ger* in the city, the language used implies that he has established a special relation with the people of Gibeah and is entitled to call the men "brothers." This however does not in any way suffice and the pressure of the men forces an alternative option. The old man is clearly mistaken in the conclusion that he speaks a language which is the same as that of the Gibeahites. One might say that the old man and the Levite entered into a conversation where they did not know the language. To be sure it was a language of violence, but the dominant expression of such violence was against the stranger, the Levite.[36] Whether the nationality and geographical origin of the old man make any difference here is immaterial and in fact the tone that is

---

35. Niditch, "The 'Sodomite' Theme" 369, makes an interesting and helpful parallel in seeking to place the issue of homosexual rape in context. She notes, "The threat of homosexual rape is . . . a potent symbol of acultural, non-civilized behavior from the Israelite point of view. It is an active aggressive form of inhospitality. This threat . . . can be compared with Homer's use of cannibalism in the Cyclopes and Laestrygones incidents of the Odyssey."

36. See Brueggemann, "The Legitimacy of a Sectarian Hermeneutic," who proposes a very useful and instructive metaphor of language "on the wall." Both the old man and the Levite were *gerim* (vv. 1, 6) and they indeed spoke a "foreign" language. They were prompted not by a legitimate "sectarian hermeneutic" as Brueggemann proposes, but sought to negotiate on the level of the men of Gibeah. The result as if to testify to the gravity of the error, is horrific violence.

set makes it clear that the men of the city had made up their minds and the meekly articulated petition to them did not change their minds. The old man seeks to have the men of the city recognize two factors: this is a wicked thing to do and guests cannot be treated in this ill manner. Both factors are very important, but the old man lacking the strength, mental or otherwise, to oppose the men of the city, and without pursuing his acknowledged moral position to any length, abandons this direction and takes up another. The alternative proves fatal.[37] Before summarily dismissing the old man as evil or inhumane, we should at least note that he had the right intentions; hence the ensuing act raises critical and deep rooted questions. There are several factors to note here.

First, the argument of the host hinges on the fact that these people are his house guests and consequently he seeks to protect them with all his power. To be sure this might appear noble and if pursued to the logical end, arguably the end result might very well have been the same. That however is not the case as he easily abandons this *modus operandi*.

Second, if it is a male person that the men of Gibeah are seeking, then why is the servant not offered.[38] This is hardly a noble suggestion, for it defeats the purpose of the old man. However by not offering the servant the actions of the old man, and indeed the Levite are seriously called into question to critical scrutiny. In effect what has happened here is that the woman and the virgin daughter are treated as property valued less than servants. Though the real interest of the men of the city was in the Levite, the women are offered as less than ideal, though disposable substitutes.[39] The reality is that the women are treated with absolute disrespect and lack of any care for their humanity. Moreover the combination of a virgin and a concubine serves to underline the

---

37. Speaking to the connection between Genesis 19 and Judges 19, Alter observes that in Genesis 19, "The host has but one virgin daughter to offer to the mob in place of the demanded male visitor, and so he makes up the tally of two proffered women by adding the visitor's concubine. This being a version of Sodom without divine intervention, the denouement is grimmer. The visitor is no angel in any sense of the term, and instead of striking the assailants with blindness, he thrusts his concubine out into the street where she is gang-raped all night long." "Sodom as Nexus," 158.

38. Trible, *Texts of Terror*, 75, correctly points out that in the Lot narrative and Judges 19, the one constant is, "the use of innocent and helpless women to guard and gratify men of all sorts."

39. Ibid., 74: "conflict among [males] can be solved by the sacrifice of females." Also, Lerner, *The Creation of Patriarchy*, 174, who observes that "the text assumes that no explanation for such behavior is necessary."

spectrum of women, who, regardless of their particular station in life or their marital status, are deemed disposable.[40] Gerda Lerner notes that, "The virgin daughters are as disposable as the concubine or the enslaved women captured in warfare."[41] If the old man were so intent on protecting all the guests in his house, then why should the women be made available to the violent men of the city? Moreover, the men of Gibeah would not listen to the offer of the women.

Third, given the fact that the old man seeks to avoid violence and evil against the guests, then it is even more striking that his substitute utterly defeats his original intent. In plain terms he simply substitutes one expression of violence for another. To go even further with this, one is led to believe that the old man and the Levite convince the men of the city that they should in fact rape the women. Not only are the women made available to the men, but in fact they are encouraged to rape and abuse the women.[42] The old man invites the men to do this and the Levite pushes the reluctant woman out of the door and closes it behind her. Any inkling that the Levite was transformed and had a change of heart when he went to convince the woman to return to him, is dashed, as he makes the final move towards absolutely destroying and finally killing his partner. To the extent that the Levite was responsible for the violence to the woman which resulted in her death, he is not a whit different from the men of Gibeah. James Nelson alerts us to the capacious and rich meanings associated with *yadaʿ*. On the one hand it has to do with sexual desire, but equally important it has to do with knowledge of the person who one desires. According to Nelson: "If I desire another sexually without wanting deep personal knowledge or living communion with my partner, then I treat the other as object, as means to my own gratification. But in the union of desiring and knowing, I treat my

---

40. Seeking to create a material difference in the actions of Lot and the Gibeah host, Lasine ("Guest and Host in Judges 19," 39) argues, "It is one thing to offer one's daughter to a mob in order to fulfill one's duty as host, and another to offer one's virgin daughter and the concubine of one's guest! The words and actions of the old host are almost identical to those of Lot at this point, but their effect is to invert Lot's overblown hospitality into inhospitality." The distinction Lasine seeks to draw here eludes me.

41. Lerner, *The Creation of Patriarchy*, 175 (cf. Amos 1:13).

42. While the NRSV uses "ravish," the Hebrew term used here is *ʿinnah* which is the term used to describe the rape of Dinah (Gen 34:2) and the rape of Tamar (2 Sam 13:12, 14).

partner as a self, the treasured participant in communion."[43] Among the elements in common between the Levite and the men of Gibeah is the fact that neither had an interest in the union of desiring and knowing. The separation of the two results in death.

In this respect, it is revealing to discover the narrator's sharp contrast of the manner in which the Levite is welcomed in the house of the woman's father and the emotions there; he is further welcomed into the house of the old man. Finally we note the manner in which the Levite accommodates the woman in the face of death.

19:3	The woman brought him in the house of the father
	The father . . . saw him . . . rejoiced.
19:20	So he [old man] brought him into the house
	they washed their feet; they ate and drank.
19:25	The Levite pushed her out of the house
	. . . They raped her and abused her.

To miss this connection between the different expressions of hospitality is to miss the essence of the narrative. In the first instance, the Levite is given life by the woman and her father, as well as by the old man, while in the third encounter, the Levite and the old man bring death to the woman. Hospitality is linked with matters of life and death!

The fact that the virgin daughter is not raped and abused is immaterial, because for all practical purposes, the offer of the father surely is tantamount to rape. In any language this is gang rape and it goes on throughout the night. This is the endorsed substitute of the men of the house. On the one hand while the pursuit of hospitality at all costs is lauded, the double violence committed as a substitute is reprehensible.[44]

Once again, we are confronted with darkness. Here, the darkness serves to shield the evil of the men. Violence and rape are committed during the darkness, and once the light comes, the deed is completed. Verse 26 moves the scene out of darkness into light. The deed was first hatched in the darkness of the hearts of evil men and then propounded by the darkness of the old man and the Levite.

---

43. Nelson, *Between Two Gardens*, 10.

44. See McKenzie, *The World of the Judges*, 165, observes that "The duty of the host to protect the guest we can understand, but not to the point where the honor and life of the women of the family are regarded as expendable. That the women should be sacrificed to save the man was taken for granted."

The extreme and brutal violence of the act is given sharper and profound intensity by the narrator as the darkness motif is continued. The woman is raped and abused throughout the night (v. 25, *kol-hallaylah*), that is while it was dark. The emphasis on the lengthy and continual violence against the totally abandoned woman creates in the minds of the readers the absolute disregard for the humanity of the woman.[45] The old man and the Levite's invitation to the men of the city to rape and abuse the woman made clear that the issue at stake was entirely sexual violence. The only two people who were even remotely capable of advocating on behalf of the woman in fact chose the worst possible alternative and disposed of her in a fashion unworthy of any piece of property. The structure of vv. 26–27 aid in the narrator's intent.

> v. 26 As morning appeared—A
>   The woman came and fell down—B
>   It was light—C
> v. 27 In the morning—A'
>   The master arose and . . . went out—B'

The dramatic contrast in these verses creates a motif of life and death, where again the temporal motif is used effectively. In this instance however, it is not the darkness which has so dominated the scene that stands out but the light. The actions of the Levite and the presence of the battered woman are both revealed in the light of the day. While the narrative pronounces that the men of Gibeah raped and killed the woman, the presence of the woman on the threshold of the man's house would remind us that the Levite must take the responsibility.[46] The situation of the Levite is in sharp contrast with the woman. The use of light in this instance serves as the central counterpoint to the role of dark-

---

45. See Bal, *Death and Dissymmetry*, 71, perceptively uses the military imagery of *Veni, vidi, vici* to speak of rape. Surely this military imagery describes with uncanny precision the man's actions against the woman.

46. Niditch, "The 'Sodomite' Theme," 371, correctly places the marginality of the woman in a larger framework; she argues that "The man's insensitivity towards his concubine, his non-communication with her, his selfishness are in fact a microcosm of larger community-relationships in Israel. He does not take care of her, the townspeople do not take care of him, men of the town are openly hostile in an exemplary antisocial, uncivilized way." This observation reflects well the concluding and indicting pronouncement, "In those days there was no king in Israel; all the people did what was right in their own eyes" (Judg 21:25). These words set the stage for the disintegration of the moral and ethical fibers of society.

ness that brought violence and death. Now the light seeks to reveal to the Levite the extent to which his actions have caused death and irreparable damage, though it is not at all certain that this revelation affects the Levite. The narrator also gives a clear indication that the Levite not only slept through the whole ordeal, but in reality had no interest in the welfare of the woman. Verse 27 captures the essence of the Levite's attitude: "he went out to go on his way, and there was his concubine lying at the door of the house." There is no intimation in the description that the Levite was planning to take the woman along with him. The matter of speaking to her heart to be reunited with her, is absent here. There is the underlying assumption that not only did he not plan to be with the concubine for the remainder of the journey, but also, he was surprised to find her on the doorsteps. The use of *hinneh* in the context alerts us to this. He had assumed her death or at least her absence and therefore was planning to leave without her.

Moreover the particularity of the woman's, "falling down" and the Levite's "rising up" function as a point of transformation as it becomes a metaphor for a larger issue. The matter of life and death is brought into sharp focus here and what began as hospitality resulted in the rape and death of an innocent and marginal person.[47] Hospitality must never under any circumstances lead to this. "Rising up" has to do with life and "falling down" with death.

Further, the brutality of the men's rape and abuse is matched with the crude uncaring manner of the Levite.[48] One would have thought that there would be an element of concern for the woman given the circumstances of the previous evening and the state in which she finds herself the following morning. As if to intensify the point of utter lack of concern for the woman, the narrator has the Levite demonstrate absolutely no emotion on the sight of the woman. There is no kneeling

---

47. See Bal, "The Rape of Narrative and the Narrative of Rape," 17, insightfully observes: "The hands on the threshold that both accuse and implore are ignored by the husband to whom they are addressed. Beth's [Bal's ascribed name for the anonymous woman] claim to safety in the house is countered by the husband's final attempt to take her to *his* house."

48. Lerner, *The Creation of Patriarchy*, 174, maintains that, "Throughout, it is clear that the insult and the 'wickedness' was the crime of inhospitality and the despoiling of the Levite's honor and property. The Levite's attitude toward his concubine . . . shows not only in his willingness to surrender her to gang rape but in his sleeping peacefully during the night of her ordeal."

over her; there is no reaching down to meet her at the threshold. There is simply the command from on high, "get up." If anything, there is the ironic use of *qumi* (v. 28), which is the same term used for the arising of the Levite from the night rest, *vayyaqom* (v. 27).[49] The narrator's use of the imperative of this Hebrew root as the Levite commands the woman to arise reminds us that this Levite was totally incapable of bringing life again to this woman. His command to do so will prove to be worthless. But the insensitivity of the Levite stands in the broad daylight for everyone to see.[50] As part of the narrator's intent, the conclusion with regard to the woman's state of being is open ended. The readers will have to draw their own conclusion. The issue here is not that the narrator is seeking to hide the death of the woman, for surely the Levite recognizes this and consequently places her on the donkey. But there is no tear shed.

The fact that in death the woman would teach a painful lesson to the Israelites is surely important, but this lesson hardly justifies the violence she suffered. The three imperatives used in v. 30 are all essential for hospitality. If anything all three of these essential characteristics were absent from the old man and Levite in their encounter with the men of Gibeah. While for a complete relationship, *dbr* and *šmʿ* must be inseparable, the absence of the latter (v. 25a) must not deter from the act of speaking. The irony must not be missed, for surely it is through the spoken word that life was brought into being (Genesis 1). The implications for contemporary believers are startling. In the face of violence against the marginalized and innocent, the voice of the people must not be kept still. For those who would remove their voices in the face of violence have in fact participated in the violence (see Obadiah 10-12). The words attributed to Martin Niemöller, German Lutheran pastor

---

49. One's attention is directed to the raising of the daughter of Jairus where similar language is used by Jesus but with deep empathy, the words take on a different tone and their pronouncement bring life to the little girl.(Mark 5:41)

50. See Unterman, "Sternberg's Ambiguity and the Bible's," 204-5, concludes, "The Levite sufficiently arouses our revulsion by his indifference to the fate of the concubine when he throws her to the wolves. By that action alone he is responsible for her murder. By the time he heartlessly orders her to get up in the morning, she is obviously dead. It is interesting that the use of ʿ*nh* in 19:28 provides us with a brutal ironic pun on 'torture' *wʿnw* in 19:24—a pun which is chiastically repeated when, to the people's query, the Levite 'answered' (*wyʿn*, 20:4) so smoothly, 'they tortured her' (ʿ*nw*, 20:5). His answer seeks to absolve himself of any culpability. Her answer is silence, but the silence strikes in our memory."

who was held prisoner—first at Sachsenhausen, then at Dachau—in Nazi Germany are instructive here:

> First they came for the Jews
> and I did not speak out—
> Because I was not a Jew.
>
> Then they came for the communists
> and I did not speak out—
> because I was not a communist.
>
> Then they came for the trade unionists
> and I did not speak out—
> because I was not a trade unionist.
>
> Then they came for me—
> And there was no one left to speak out for me![51]

---

51. The exact wording of this quotation has been widely debated, including the groups to which Niemöller referred. See Prof. Harold Marcuse's Web site, "Martin Niemöller's Famous Quotation": http://www.history.ucsb.edu/faculty/marcuse/niem.htm.

Bibliography

Achtemeier, Elizabeth R. "Righteousness in the OT." In *Interpreter's Dictionary of the Bible*, edited by George Arthur Buttrick, 80–85. Nashville: Abingdon, 1962.
Alexander, Desmond T. "Lot's Hospitality: A Clue to His Righteousness." *JBL* 104 (1985) 289–91.
Alter, Robert. "Sodom as Nexus: The Web of Design in Biblical Narrative." In *The Book and the Text: The Bible and Literary Theory*, edited by Regina Schwartz, 146–60. Oxford: Blackwell, 1990.
Auerbach, Erich. *Mimesis: The Representation of Reality in Western Literature*. Princeton: Princeton University Press, 1953.
Bailey, D. Sherwin. *Homosexuality and the Western Christian Tradition*. London: Longman, Green, 1955.
Bal, Mieke. *Death and Dissymmetry: The Politics of Coherence in the Book of Judges*. Chicago Studies in the History of Judaism. Chicago: University of Chicago Press, 1988.
―――. "The Rape of Narrative and the Narrative of Rape." In *Literature and the Body: Essays on Populations and Person*, edited by Elaine Scarry, 1–32. Baltimore: Johns Hopkins University Press, 1988.
Bettenhausen, Elizabeth. "Hagar Revisited: Surrogacy, Alienation and Motherhood." *Christianity and Crisis* 47.7 (1987) 157–59.
Bodoff, Lipmann. "The Real Test of the *Akedah*: Blind Obedience versus Moral Choice." *Judaism* 42 (1993) 71–92.
Boff, Leonardo. *Church, Charism and Power: Liberation Theology and the Institutional Church*. Translated by John Diercksmeier. New York: Crossroad, 1986.
Boling, Robert G. *Judges*. Anchor Bible 7. Doubleday, 1975.
Breech, James. *The Silence of Jesus: The Authentic Voice of the Historical Man*. Philadelphia: Fortress, 1983.
―――. *Jesus and Postmodernism*. Minneapolis: Fortress, 1989.
Breithart, Sidney. "The Akedah: A Test of God." *Dor le Dor* 15.1 (1986) 19–28.
Brisman, Leslie. *The Voice of Jacob: On the Composition of Genesis*. ISBL. Bloomington: Indiana University Press, 1990.
Brock, Rita Nakashima. *Journeys by Heart: A Christology of Erotic Power*. New York: Crossroad, 1991.
Brueggemann, Walter. "Canonization and Contextualization." In *Interpretation and Obedience: From Faithful Reading to Faithful Living*, edited by Patrick D. Miller, 119–42. Minneapolis: Fortress, 1991.
―――. *Genesis*. Interpretation. Atlanta: John Knox, 1982.
―――. "'Impossibility' and Epistemology in the Faith Tradition of Abraham and Sarah (Gen. 18:1–15)." *ZAW* 94 (1982) 615–34.

———. "Land, Fertility and Justice." In *Theology of the Land*, edited by Bernard F. Evans and Gregory Cusack, 41–68. Collegeville, MN: Liturgical, 1987.

———. "The Legitimacy of a Sectarian Hermeneutic." *HBT* 7 (1985) 1–42.

———. *Power, Providence and Personality*. Louisville: Westminster John Knox, 1990.

———. "Preaching to the Exiles." *Journal of Preaching* 16.4 (1993) 3–15.

———. "The Transformative Potential of a Public Metaphor." In *Interpretation and Obedience: From Faithful Reading to Faithful Living*, edited by Patrick Miller, 70–99. Fortress, 1991.

Buechner, Frederick. *Peculiar Treasures: A Biblical Who's Who*. New York: Harper & Row, 1979.

Carmichael, Calum M. *Law and Narrative in the Bible: The Evidence of the Deuteronomic Laws and the Decalogue*. 1985. Reprint, Eugene, OR: Wipf & Stock, 2008.

Chopp, Rebecca. *The Power to Speak: Feminism, Language, God*. New York: Crossroad, 1989.

Clark, Elizabeth, and Herbert Richardson. "The *Malleus Maleficarum*: The Woman as Witch." In *Women and Religion: A Feminist Sourcebook of Christian Thought*, edited by Elizabeth Clark and Herbert Richardson, 116–30. New York: Harper & Row, 1977.

Clines, David J. A. "The Ancestor in Danger: But Not the Same Danger." In *What Does Eve Do to Help? And Other Readerly Questions in the Old Testament*, 67–84. JSOTSup 94. Sheffield: JSOT Press, 1990.

Coats, George W. *Genesis: With an Introduction to Narrative Literature*. Forms of the Old Testament Literature 1. Grand Rapids: Eerdmans, 1983.

———. "Lot: A Foil in the Abraham Narrative." In *Understanding the Word: Essays in Honor of Bernhard W. Anderson*, edited by James T. Butler et al., 113–32. JSOTSup 37. Sheffield: JSOT, 1985.

———. "A Threat to the Host." In *Saga, Legend, Tale, Novella, Fable: Narrative Forms in Old Testament Literature*, edited by George W. Coats, 71–81. JSOTSup 35. Sheffield: JSOT Press, 1985.

Collins, Mary. "Naming God in Public Prayer." *Worship* 59 (1985) 291–304.

Crenshaw, James L. "A Monstrous Test: Genesis 22." In *A Whirlpool of Torment: Israelite Traditions of God as an Oppressive Presence*, 9–29. OBT. Minneapolis: Fortress, 1985.

———. "Journey into Oblivion: A Structures Analysis." *Soundings* 58 (1975) 243–56.

Croatto, J. Severino. *Exodus: A Hermeneutics of Freedom*. Translated by Salvator Attanasio. Maryknoll, NY: Orbis, 1981.

Dahl, Nils Alstrup. *Jesus the Christ: The Historical Origins of Christological Doctrine*. Edited by Donald H. Juel. Minneapolis: Fortress, 1991.

Darr, Katheryn Pfisterer. *Far More Precious Than Jewels: Perspectives on Biblical Women*. Gender and the Biblical Tradition. Philadelphia: Westminster, 1991.

De Jong, Meindert. *The Wheel on the School*. Pictures by Maurice Sendak. New York: Harper & Row, 1954.

Dillmann, August. *Genesis: Critically and Exegetically Expounded*. 2 vols. Edinburgh: T. & T. Clark, 1897.

Doig, Desmond. *Mother Teresa: Her People and Her Work*. San Francisco: Harper & Row, 1976.

Fretheim, Terence E. *Abraham: Trials of Family and Faith*. Studies on Personalities of the Old Testament. Columbia: University of South Carolina Press, 2007.
———. *Exodus*. Interpretation. Atlanta: John Knox, 1991.
———. "Prayer in the Old Testament: Creating Space in the World for God." In *Primer on Prayer*, edited by Paul R. Sponheim, 51–62. Philadelphia: Fortress, 1988.
———. *The Suffering of God*. OBT. Philadelphia: Fortress, 1984.
Fuchs, Esther. "The Literary Characterization of Mothers and Sexual Politics in the Hebrew Bible." In *Feminist Perspectives on Biblical Scholarship*, edited by Adela Yarbro Collins, 117–36. Biblical Scholarship in North America. Scholars, 1985. Reprinted in Alice Bach, editor, *Women in the Hebrew Bible: A Reader*, edited by Alice Bach, 127–39. London: Routledge, 1999.
Gaiser, Fred. "Homosexuality and the Old Testament." *WW* (1990) 161–65.
Gammie, John G. *Holiness in Israel*. OBT. Minneapolis: Fortress, 1989.
Gamoran, Hillel. "The Biblical Law against Loans on Interest." *Journal of Near Eastern Studies*. 30 (1971) 127–34.
Gossai, Hemchand. *Barrenness and Blessing: Abraham, Sarah and the Journey of Faith*. Eugene, OR: Cascade Books. 2008.
———. *Social Critique by Israel's Eighth Century Prophets: Justice and Righteousness in Context*. 1993. Reprinted, Eugene, OR: Wipf & Stock, 2006.
Gunkel, Herman. *The Legends of Genesis*. Translated by W. H. Carruth. New York: Schocken, 1964.
Gutierrez, Gustavo. *The Power of the Poor in History*. Translated by Robert R. Barr. Maryknoll, NY: Orbis, 1983.
———. *On Job: God-Talk and the Suffering of the Innocent*. Translated by Matthew J. O'Connell. Maryknoll, NY: Orbis, 1987.
Hackett, JoAnn. "Rehabilitating Hagar: Fragments of an Epic Pattern." In *Gender and Difference in Ancient Israel*, edited by Peggy L. Day, 12–27. Minneapolis: Fortress, 1989.
Hall, Douglas John. *The Stewardship of Life in the Kingdom of Death*. Grand Rapids: Eerdmans, 1988.
Hampson, Daphne. "On Power and Gender." *Modern Theology* 4 (1988) 234–50.
Haughton, Rosemary. *The Passionate God*. Mahwah, NJ: Paulist, 1981.
Heger, Heinz. *The Men with the Pink Triangle*. Translated by David Fernbach. London: Gay Men's Press, 1980.
Hemans, Felicia Dorothea. "Casabianca." *Monthly Magazine* (August 1826). Reprinted in *The Poetical Works of Felicia Dorothea Hemans*, 396. London: Oxford University Press, 1914.
Herzfeld, Michael. "'As in Your House': Hospitality, Ethnography, and the Stereotype of Mediterranean Society." In *Honor and Shame and the Unity of the Mediterranean*, edited by David G. Gilmore, 75–87. Washington, DC: American Anthropological Society, 1987.
Heyward, Carter. *The Redemption of God: A Theology of Mutual Relation*. Washington, DC: University Press of America, 1983.
hooks, bell. *Feminist Theory: From Margin to Center*. Boston: South End, 1984.
Humphreys, W. Lee. *The Tragic Vision and the Hebrew Tradition*. OBT. Minneapolis: Fortress, 1985.

Janzen, J. Gerald. "Hagar in Paul's Eyes and in the Eyes of Yahweh (Genesis 16): A Study in Horizons." *HBT* 13 (1991) 1-22.
Jeansonne, Sharon Pace. *The Women of Genesis*. Minneapolis: Fortress, 1990.
Johnson, Elizabeth A. *She Who Is: The Mystery of God in Feminist Theological Discourse*. New York: Crossroad, 1992.
Jung, C. G. *Answer to Job*. Princeton: Princeton University Press, 1969.
———. *Memories, Dreams, Reflections*. Edited by Aniela Jaffé. Translated by Richard and Clara Winston. New York: Vintage, 1989.
Jungling, Hans-Winfried. *Richter 19—Ein Pladoyer für das Königtum*. Analecta biblica 84. Rome: Biblical Institute Press, 1981.
Kierkegaard, Søren. *Fear and Trembling: A Dialectical Lyric*. Translated by Walter Lowrie. Princeton: Princeton University Press, 1941.
Klein, Lillian R. *The Triumph of Irony in the Book of Judges*. JSOTSup 68. Sheffield: Almond, 1988.
Koch, Klaus. *The Growth of the Biblical Tradition: The Form-Critical Method*. Translated by S. M. Cupitt. New York: Scribner, 1969.
Kohn, Murray J. "The Trauma of Isaac." *Jewish Biblical Quarterly* (1991-92) 96-104.
Koyama, Kosuke. *Three Mile an Hour God: Biblical Reflections*. Maryknoll, NY: Orbis, 1979.
Lasine, Stuart. "Guest and Host in Judges 19: Lot's Hospitality in an Inverted World." *JSOT* 29 (1984) 37-59.
Lerner, Gerda. *The Creation of Patriarchy*. Oxford University Press, 1986.
Luther, Martin. *Lectures on Genesis 15-20*. Edited by Jaroslav Pelikan. St. Louis: Concordia, 1961.
Mabee, Charles. *Reimagining America: A Theological Critique of the American Mythos and Biblical Hermeneutics*. Studies in American Biblical Hermeneutics 1. Macon, GA: Mercer University Press, 1985.
Marks, John. "The Book of Genesis." *The Interpreter's One-Volume Commentary on the Bible*, edited by Charles M. Laymon, 1-32. Nashville: Abingdon, 1973.
Marmesh, Ann. "Anti-Covenant." In *Anti-Covenant: Counter Readings Women's Lives in the Hebrew Bible*, edited by Mieke Bal, 43-58. JSOTSup 81. Sheffield: Almond, 1989.
Martin, James D. *The Book of Judges*. Cambridge: Cambridge University Press, 1975.
Martinson, Paul V. "The Crucified and Risen Buddha? A Question of Finality." *WW* 9 (1989) 224-35.
Matthews, Victor H. "Hospitality and Hostility in Genesis 19 and Judges 19." *Biblical Theology Bulletin* 22 (1992) 3-11.
McKenzie, John L. *The World of the Judges*. Englewood Cliffs, NJ: Prentice Hall, 1966.
Milgrom, Jacob. "The Biblical Diet Laws as an Ethical System: Food and Faith." *Int* 17 (1963) 288-301.
Miller, Jerome A. *The Way of Suffering: A Geography of Crisis*. Washington, DC: Georgetown University Press, 1988.
Miscall, Peter. "Literary Unity in Old Testament Narrative." *Semeia* 15 (1979) 27-44.
Moberly, R. W. L. *From Eden to Golgotha: Essays in Biblical Theology*. South Florida Studies in the History of Judaism 52. Atlanta: Scholars, 1992.
Moster, Julius. "The Testing of Abraham." *Dor le Dor* 17 (1989) 237-42.
Muecke, D. C. *The Compass of Irony*. London: Methuen, 1969.

Nelson, James B. *Between Two Gardens: Reflections on Sexuality and Religious Experience*. Cleveland: Pilgrim, 1983.

Neufeld, Edward. "The Prohibitions against Loans at Interest in Ancient Hebrew Laws." *Hebrew Union College Annual* 26 (1955) 355–412.

Niditch, Susan. "The 'Sodomite' Theme in Judges 19–20: Family, Community and Social Disintegration." *Catholic Biblical Quarterly* 44 (1982) 365–78.

———. *Underdogs and Tricksters: A Prelude to Biblical Folklore*. New Voices in Biblical Studies. San Francisco: Harper & Row, 1987.

Noth, Martin. *A History of Pentateuchal Traditions*. Translated by Bernhard W. Anderson. Englewood Cliffs, NJ: Prentice Hall, 1972.

Nouwen, Henri. *The Wounded Healer: Ministry in Contemporary Society*. Garden City, NY: Doubleday, 1972.

Ogletree, Thomas. *Hospitality to the Stranger: Dimensions of Moral Understanding*. Minneapolis: Fortress, 1985.

Palmer, Parker J. *The Company of Strangers: Christians and the Renewal of America's Public Life*. New York: Crossroad, 1991.

Patrick, Dale. *The Rendering of God in the Old Testament*. OBT. Minneapolis: Fortress, 1981.

Peterson, David L. "A Thrice-Told Tale: Genre, Theme and Motif." *Papers of the Chicago Society of Biblical Research* 18 (1973) 30–41.

Plank, Karl. "The Survivor's Return: Reflections on Memory and Place." *Judaism* 38 (1989) 263–77.

Polzin, Robert. "'The Ancestress of Israel in Danger' in Danger." *Semeia* 3 (1975) 81–98.

Rad, Gerhard von. *Old Testament Theology*. Vol. 1, *The Theology of Israel's Historical Traditions*. Translated by D. M. G. Stalker. New York: Harper & Row, 1965.

Rosenberg, Joel. *King and Kin: Political Allegory in the Hebrew Bible*. ISBL. Bloomington: Indiana University Press, 1986.

Sakenfeld, Katherine Doob. *Faithfulness in Action: Loyalty in Biblical Perspective*. OBT. Minneapolis: Fortress, 1985.

Sarna, Nahum. *Understanding Genesis: The Heritage of Biblical Israel*. New York: Schocken, 1966.

———. *Genesis*. JPS Torah Commentary. New York: Jewish Publication Society, 1989.

Scanzoni, Letha, and Virginia Ramey Molenkott. *Is the Homosexual My Neighbor?* San Francisco: Harper & Row, 1978.

Schutz, Alfred. *Collected Papers: Studies in Social Theory II*. Edited by Arvid Brodersen. Phaenomonologica 15. The Hague: Nijhoff, 1976.

Schüssler Fiorenza, Elisabeth. "Emerging Issues in Feminist Biblical Interpretation." In *Christian Feminism: Visions of a New Humanity*, edited by Judith L. Weidman, 33–54. San Francisco: Harper & Row, 1984.

Skinner, John. *A Critical and Exegetical Commentary on the Book of Genesis*. International Critical Commentary. T. & T. Clark, 1910.

Soelle, Dorothee. *Death by Bread Alone: Texts and Reflections on Religious Experience*. Translated by David L. Scheidt. Philadelphia: Fortress, 1978.

———. *Thinking about God: An Introduction to Theology*. Translated by John Bowden. Philadelphia: Trinity, 1990.

———, with Shirley Cloyes. *To Work and to Love: A Theology of Creation.* Philadelphia: Fortress, 1984.
Soggin, Alberto J. *Judges.* Translated by John Bowden. Old Testament Library. Philadelphia: Westminster, 1981.
Speiser, E. A. *Genesis.* Anchor Bible 1. Garden City, NY: Doubleday, 1964.
Stegner, William Richard. *Narrative Theology in Early Jewish Christianity.* Louisville: Westminster John Knox, 1989.
Steinmetz, Devora. *From Father to Son: Kinship, Conflict, and Continuity in Genesis.* Literary Currents in Biblical Interpretation. Louisville: Westminster John Knox, 1991.
Sternberg, Meir. *The Poetics of Biblical Narrative: Ideological Literature and the Drama of Reading.* ISBL. Bloomington: Indiana University Press, 1985.
Strauss, Leo. "The Beginning of the Bible and Its Greek Counterparts." In *Genesis*, edited by Harold Bloom. Modern Critical Interpretations. New York: Chelsea House, 1986.
Suchocki, Marjorie Hewitt. "In Search of Justice." In *The Myth of Christian Uniqueness: Toward a Pluralistic Theology of Religions*, edited by John Hick and Paul Knitter, 150–54. Maryknoll, NY: Orbis, 1987.
Tamez, Elsa. *Bible of the Oppressed.* Translated by Matthew J. O'Connell. Maryknoll, NY: Orbis, 1982.
———. "The Woman Who Complicated the History of Salvation." In *New Eyes for Reading: Biblical and Theological Reflections by Women from the Third World*, edited John Pobee and Barbel von Wartenberg-Potter, 5–17. Geneva: World Council of Churches, 1986.
Tapp, Anne Michele. "An Ideology of Expendability: Virgin Daughter Sacrifice in Genesis 19:1–11, Judges 11:30–39 and 19:22–26." In *Anti-Covenant: Counter Reading Women's Lives in the Hebrew Bible*, edited by Mieke Bal, 157–74. JSOTSup 81. Sheffield: Sheffield Academic, 1989.
Tarlo, Peter E., and E. Cleve Want. "Bad Guys, Textual Errors and Word Plays in Genesis 21:9–10." *Journal of Reformed Judaism* 37.4 (1990) 21–28.
Terrien, Samuel. *The Elusive Presence: Toward a New Biblical Theology.* 1978. Reprinted, Eugene, OR: Wipf & Stock, 2000.
Teubal, Savina J. *Hagar the Egyptian: The Lost Tradition of the Matriarchs.* San Francisco: Harper & Row, 1990.
Tillich, Paul. *Theology of Culture.* Oxford: Oxford University Press, 1959.
Trible, Phyllis. "Genesis 22: The Sacrifice of Sarah." In *Not in Heaven: Coherence and Complexity in Biblical Narrative*, edited by Jason P. Rosenblatt and Joseph C. Sitterson Jr., 170–91. ISBL. Bloomington: Indiana University Press, 1991.
———. *God and the Rhetoric of Sexuality.* OBT. Philadelphia: Fortress, 1978.
———. *Texts of Terror: Literary Feminist Readings of the Biblical Narratives.* OBT. Minneapolis: Fortress, 1984.
Tsevat, Matitiahu. *The Meaning of the Book of Job and Other Biblical Studies: Essays on the Literature and Religion of the Hebrew Bible.* New York: Ktav, 1980.
Turner, Lawrence A. *Announcements of Plot in Genesis.* JSOTSup 96. Sheffield: JSOT Press, 1990.
Unterman, Jeremiah. "Sternberg's Ambiguity and the Bible's: With an Appendix on the Non-ambiguity of the Killing of the Concubine (Judges 19:30)." *Hebrew Studies* 29 (1988) 208–9.

Van Seters, John. *Abraham in History and Tradition*. New Haven: Yale University Press, 1975.

Vaux, Roland de. *Ancient Israel: Its Life and Institutions*. Translated by John McHugh. London: Darton, Longman & Todd, 1961.

Vermes, Geza. *Scripture and Tradition in Judaism*. Studia post-Biblica 4. Leiden: Brill, 1973.

Waters, John. "Who Was Hagar?" In *Stony the Road We Trod: African American Biblical Interpretation*, edited by Cain Hope Felder, 187–205. Minneapolis: Fortress, 1991.

Weems, Renita J. *Just a Sister Away: A Womanist Vision of Women's Relationship in the Bible*. San Diego: Luramedia, 1988.

Weil, Simone. *Waiting for God*. Translated by Emma Craufurd. New York: Harper & Row, 1951.

Westermann, Claus. *Genesis 12–36*. Translated by John J. Scullion. Continental Commentaries. Minneapolis: Augsburg, 1985.

White, Hugh C. *Narration and Discourse in the Book of Genesis*. Cambridge: Cambridge University Press, 1991.

Wiesel, Elie. Interview with Bill Moyers. *Beyond Hate*. PBS. May 13, 1991.

———."Ishmael and Hagar." In *The Life of Covenant: The Challenge of Contemporary Judaism*, edited by Joseph A. Edelheit, 235–49. Chicago: Spertus College of Judaica Press, 1986.

———. *Night*. Translated by Stella Rodway. New York: Hill & Wang, 1960.

———. "The Sacrifice of Isaac: A Survivor's Story." In *Messengers of God: Biblical Portraits and Legends*, 69–97. New York: Random House, 1976.

———. *Twilight*. Translated by Marion Wiesel. New York: Summit, 1988.

Wiesner, Merry E. "Luther and Women: The Death of Two Mary's." In *Feminist Theology: A Reader*, edited by Ann Loades, 123–37. Philadelphia: Westminster, 1990.

Wilbur, Richard. "A Stable Lamp Is Lighted." In *Lutheran Book of Worship*. Minneapolis: Augsburg, 1978.

Wolff, Hans Walter. "The Elohistic Fragments in the Pentateuch." *Int* 26 (1972) 161–63.

Yeres, Moshe. "The Meaning of Abraham's Test: A Reexamination of the Akedah." *Dor le Dor* 19.1 (1990) 3–10.

www.ingramcontent.com/pod-product-compliance
Lightning Source LLC
Chambersburg PA
CBHW051939160426
43198CB00013B/2225